The well-managed classroom for Catholic schools

Also from the Boys Town Press

Books

Teaching Social Skills to Youth
Basic Social Skills for Youth
Common Sense Parenting®, 2nd Edition
Unmasking Sexual Con Games: Helping Teens Identify Good and Bad Relationships
The Ongoing Journey: Awakening Spiritual Life in At-Risk Youth
Rebuilding Children's Lives
Building Skills in High-Risk families
Finding Happiness in Faith, Family & Work
Boys Town: A Photographic History
Boys Town Prayer Book
Working with Aggressive Youth

Videos, Audiotapes

One to One: Personal Listening Tapes for Teens
Common Sense Parenting®: Audiobook
Helping Your Child Succeed
Teaching Responsible Behavior
Videos for Parents Series
Sign With Me: A Family Sign Language Curriculum
Read With Me: Storytelling in Sign Language

For a **FREE Boys Town Press catalog**, call **1-800-282-6657.**

The well-managed classroom for Catholic schools

Promoting student success through the teaching of social skills and Christian values

▶ by Father Val J. Peter, JCD, STD
Theresa Connolly, M.A.
Tom Dowd, M.A.
Andrea Criste, M.Ed.
Cathy Nelson, M.S.
Lisa Tobias, M.S.

BOYS TOWN PRESS

BOYS TOWN, NEBRASKA

The well-managed classroom for Catholic schools

Published by The Boys Town Press
Father Flanagan's Boys' Home
Boys Town, Nebraska 68010

Publisher's Cataloging in Publication
(Prepared by Quality Books Inc.)

The Well-managed classroom for Catholic schools :
    promoting student success through the teaching
    of social skills and Christian values
    / by Father Val J. Peter . . . [et al.]. -- 1st ed.
        p. cm.
        Includes bibliographical references and index.
        ISBN 1-889322-06-7

    1. Classroom management. 2. Catholic
Church--Education. 3. Social values--Study and
teaching. 4. Christian ethics--Study and
teaching.   I. Peter, Val J.

    LB3013.W45 1998   371.1'024'08822
                             QBI97-41137

    10 9 8 7 6 5 4 3 2 1

Boys Town education training workshops

Over the past 25 years, educators have consistently identified discipline as one of the biggest problems in American schools. When educators must focus on controlling student behavior rather than teaching, learning suffers.

To solve this problem, many schools and school districts have turned to the Boys Town Education Model, a training program that enables educators to help students manage their own behavior by learning social skills.

To accomplish this goal, the Model:

– provides a step-by-step process for teaching social skills to students.

– shows educators how to make the teaching of social skills part of the regular school curriculum.

– gives educators a systematic way to address appropriate and inappropriate behavior.

– defines when and how teachers should refer students to the office.

Boys Town offers three Education Training workshops to teach these methods.

Preservice Workshops — Three workshops provides educators with the specialized technology to begin implementing the Model:

Social Skills in the Schools (three days); Comprehensive Classroom Management for Special-Needs Students (five days); and Administrative Intervention (three days).

These workshops are conducted monthly on the Boys Town Home Campus and by contract on-site throughout the country.

Consultation Services – Schools that want more than just workshop training may also contract for these services: classroom observation, treatment planning, and consultation documentation.

Training of Trainers – This training process teaches educators how to implement and supervise the Boys Town Education Model in their own schools.

Nearly 5,000 individuals from 375 schools, districts, and agencies have received training in the Boys Town Education Model. Research indicates that use of the Model helps increase the amount of time students spend on-task, and decreases the number of office referrals. Teachers spend less time dealing with disruptive behavior, and students report that they get along better with their parents, teachers, and other students.

Educators in Catholic schools who have implemented the Boys Town Education Model in their schools report overwhelmingly positive results. Clarice Franke, the principal of John Paul II Catholic School in Houston, Texas, said that "the Model was the rock upon which the positive, learning climate of the school was built. The school was named a National Blue Ribbon School of Excellence, one of only 32 private schools nationally this year. One of the major elements of the school cited in the award was the social skills model used throughout the school."

Michael Mullin, former principal of Peter, Paul, and Michael Catholic School in St. Cloud, Minnesota, said Boys Town's training is outstanding. "As a Catholic school administrator for more than 18 years, I have been to dozens of workshops and seminars regarding student behavior, many of them good and worthwhile. The Boys Town training, however, was like entering a whole new wonderful world. I think teachers feel empowered by the whole Boys Town teaching process. Knowing that there was always a formula to follow, no matter how difficult or serious the behavior, put teachers, parents, and administrators at ease. I highly recommend this program for any school that is serious about improving respect, student performance, morale, dignity, and Christian behavior."

And Larry Zahm, principal at Corpus Christi School in Fort Dodge, Iowa, said: "Through Boys Town's social skills, the students are taught the expectations of their behavior. The expectations are consistent from teacher to teacher, whether they are in the classroom or common areas. The behavior of students changes because the students know what is expected. These social skills are ones that students will continue to use throughout their lives."

Boys Town wants to share its teaching methods with you and your school. For more information about workshops, call the Boys Town Education Training program at (402) 498-1596.

Table of contents

Introduction

"The heavens declare the glory of God...."

Psalms 18

God, infinitely perfect and blessed Himself, in a plan of sheer goodness freely created man to make Him share in His own blessed life. For this reason, at every time and in every place, God draws close to man. He calls man to seek Him, to know Him, to love Him with all His strength. He calls together all men, scattered and divided by sin, into the unity of His family, the Church. To accomplish this, when the fullness of time had come, God sent His Son as Redeemer and Savior. In His Son and through Him, He invites men to become, in the Holy Spirit, His adopted children and thus heirs of His blessed life.

From the Prologue of
The Catechism of the Catholic Church

Catholic schools first appeared centuries ago, springing up outside monasteries, cathedrals, and parish churches in Europe. Generation after generation of immigrants to the United States later were taught in the parochial schools of America. The Church has always had a love for its schools, because this is where its children receive their formation. These schools have continued to flourish with the help of bishops, countless religious congregations, and laity; worldwide, the Church has never ceased to support its schools, even in difficult times, and to defend them against governments seeking to close or confiscate them.

The Catholic school receives its spirit from the Church, through which Christ's Redemption is made visible. Teachers in Catholic schools find their light and the courage to provide genuine religious education in their shared faith, beliefs, and practices. The schools' concrete educational goals include a concern for the life and the problems of the Church, both local and universal. These goals are attentive to the Magisterium, and include cooperation with Church authorities. Catholic students are helped to become active members of the parish and diocesan communities. They have opportunities to join church associations and youth groups, and they are taught to collaborate in local church projects.

Mutual esteem and reciprocal collaboration are established between the Catholic school and the bishop and other Church authorities through direct contacts. It is pleasing to note that a concern for Catholic schools is becoming more of a priority of local churches in many parts of the world.

Historically, Catholic schools were closely tied to religious women and men who educated children both in academics and the Catholic faith. Many of us attended these schools and have fond memories of these teachers. But over the past 30 years, the number of religious orders that teach in schools has diminished. The result has been a period of transition. But the goal still is to provide an excellent education with an orientation to Christian values. Teachers in Catholic schools must make a commitment to the fundamental principles of a philosophy of Catholic education in order to fulfill their roles as Catholic educators.

This introduction is designed to clarify the role of teachers in Catholic schools. Teachers have to be aware that large numbers of today's youth are worried about an uncertain future. They have been influenced by a world in which human values are in chaos because these values are no longer rooted in

God. The result is that these young people are very much afraid when they think about the appalling problems in the world: the threat of violence in the streets and at home, drugs, sex, alcohol, abuse of every kind, unemployment, the high number of marriages that end in separation or divorce, or worse yet, a widespread apathy or fatalistic view of life. Their worry and age-appropriate self-centeredness creates an irresistible urge to focus on themselves, which can result in selfishness and a trend toward violence.

In the past, Catholic communities and Church authorities were able to count on religious orders to staff and operate their primary and secondary schools. In the past 30 years, the responsibility for providing Catholic education has changed hands and we now find our students being taught by dedicated and highly motivated Catholic laity. Their commitment to their students and their schools has been laudable. It is these very same teachers who are requesting help in teaching Catholic doctrine and values in their schools. These teachers are committed to their students. They can benefit from a renewed commitment to the fundamental principles of Catholic education.

Throughout this book, teachers will be introduced to the teachings of the Catholic Church regarding the religious dimensions of education in a Catholic school. The excerpts that contain these teachings come from *The Catechetical Documents, A Parish Resource*, a book of official Church documents whose wellspring is the Second Vatican Council. (References to this material are designated by chapter titles and section numbers.) This material is included to help teachers who work in Catholic schools gain a better understanding of the fundamental principles and philosophy of Catholic schools.

Catholic philosophy of education

There are four principles that exemplify the Catholic philosophy of education: 1) the integration of religious formation and human development; 2) mediation between faith and culture; 3) enhancement of both religious and intellectual knowledge; and 4) service as an agency of public education and religious formation. Let's look at each of these in more detail. (The following numbered segments are from "The Religious Dimension of Education in a Catholic School" (1988), by the S. Congregation for Catholic Education, Rome, in *The Catechetical Documents, A Parish Resource*, pp. 488-489. Chicago: Liturgy Training Publications, 1996.)

1. Catholic schools integrate the tasks of religious formation and human development because of a Christian understanding of the fundamental unity of the human person. "The believer is both human and a person of faith, the protagonist of culture and the subject of religion." The scope of religious formation must embrace the whole of human life in a "movement or a growth process" that guides men and women to human and Christian fullness. "For those who believe in Christ, these are two facets of a single reality."

2. Catholic schools perform a "specific pastoral function" as a mediator between faith and culture. Their particular responsibility is to "interpret and give order to human culture in the light of faith." They are central to the church's educational mission, not because they merely "supplement" secular education with religious instruction, but because they are "a privileged place" where "faith, culture, and life are brought into harmony." In addition to this synthetic function, the schools also help students develop critical perspectives that enable them to "recognize and reject cultural counter-values which threaten human dignity."

3. The intellectual work and the religious work of the schools mutually enhance and illumine one another. While "being faithful to the newness of the Gospel," Catholic schools at the same time respect "the autonomy and the methods proper to human knowledge." While the academic disciplines should not be seen "merely as subservient to faith," this does not mean that "one can negate spiritual values or prescind from them."

4. The Catholic school maintains a dual identity as an agency of religious formation for life in the church and an agency of public education for life in the world. This imposes on the institution "enormous and complex" responsibilities that require careful and critical deliberation.

The Catholic school as a community

On the one hand, a Catholic school is a civic institution: Its aims, methods, and character are the same as those of every other school. On the other hand, it is a Christian community whose educational goals are rooted in Christ and His Gospel. It's not always easy to bring these two aspects into harmony; the task requires constant attention, so that the tension between a serious effort to transmit culture and forceful witness to the Gospel does not turn into a conflict that is harmful to both.

Over the years, there has been an important change in the way Catholic schools are perceived; this has been "the transition from the school as an institution to the school as a community." (The Religious Dimension of Education in a Catholic School, 31)

"This community dimension is, perhaps, one result of the new awareness of the Church's nature as developed by the (Second Vatican) Council. In the Council texts, the community dimension is primarily a theological concept rather than a sociological category; this is the sense in which it is used in the second chapter of Lumen gentium, where the Church is described as the People of God." (The Religious Dimension of Education in a Catholic School, 31)

"Everyone directly involved in the school is a part of the school community: teachers, directors, administrative and auxiliary staff. Parents are central figures, since they are the natural and irreplaceable agents in the education of their children. And the community also includes the students, since they must be active agents in their own education." (The Religious Dimension of Education in a Catholic School, 32)

It is impossible for the school as a community to develop without certain humanizing skills such as those taught by the Boys Town Model. A pile of rocks is not a community. A bunch of kids sitting at desks or even gathered in a circle without any caring or sharing is not a community. A community is characterized by:

● shared, positive experiences

● common understanding of these shared experiences

● everyone's commitment to the same goals

● daily living that reflects these experiences, understandings, and commitments

In other words, a community is a place where people care and share. In the community that is a Catholic school, this caring and sharing is rooted in the school's connection to God and the Church.

"Love for and fidelity to the Church is the organizing principle and the source of strength of a Catholic school." (The Religious Dimension of Education in a Catholic School, 44)

"While the Catholic school is like any other school in this complex variety of events that make up the life of the school, there is one essential difference: It draws its inspiration and its strength from the Gospel in which it is rooted." (The Religious Dimension of Education in a Catholic School, 47)

▶ Strategies for the mission

In order to carry out this mission of Catholic education, the Church suggests a number of concrete strategies for implementing this vision in the life and work of the school. Among its most important recommendations are the following:

(The first eight recommendations are from The Religious Dimension of Education in a Catholic School, Overview, by F.B. Veverka.)

1. A "permeation" theory of religious formation. Students entering a Catholic school should experience an educational environment "illumined by the light of faith" and "permeated with the Gospel spirit of love and freedom." Not merely an institution, the school is a "community" that gives witness to the values of "simplicity and evangelical poverty." It is not just in the teaching of religion that faith is present; teachers in other subject areas "can help students to see beyond the limited horizon of human reality.... God cannot be the Great Absent One or the unwelcome intruder."

2. The teaching of religion. Those who teach religion must be trained professionally and be competent in their task of communicating a "systemative presentation of religion. It is possible to love a person; it is rather difficult to love a formula." The authenticity of religious education is found among teachers "in their unity among themselves and their generous and humble communion with the Holy Father."

3. Recognizing the presence of non-Catholic students in Catholic schools. This underlines the need to respect the "religious freedom and personal conscience of individual students and their families." In some countries with a diverse student body, evangelization may be very difficult. The "right and duty of the school to proclaim the Gospel" is not the same as "the imposition" of faith.

4. Pursuit of social goals. Catholic schools must promote "traditional civic values such as freedom, justice, the nobility of work"; respect for the state and its laws; and commitment to social progress and the common good. At the same time, Catholic schools invite students to "develop a critical sense" so they may evaluate their world and participate in its transformation toward greater "peace, justice, freedom, and progress for all peoples."

5. Openness to a range of pedagogical theories and approaches. We need to remind ourselves "that every pedagogical current of thought contains things which are true and useful." Teachers in Catholic schools must be exposed to various approaches from which they can "begin to reflect, judge, and choose."

6. Respect for students. Catholic schools need to create a "warm and trusting atmosphere" where teachers "accept the students as they are." Teachers can establish rapport with students by being available for personal conversation and by responding to them with "affection, tact, understanding, serenity of spirit, a balanced judgment, patience... and prudence."

Along with this, every Catholic school should have and follow these two basic rules:

- Teachers and staff will not show disrespect for any students. (Kids call this "dissing.") If it appears to students that you are showing them disrespect, they should be taught how to let you know. This disrespect is almost always unintentional and will stop if students appropriately discuss the situation with a teacher or staff member.

- Students will show respect for other students, teachers, and other school staff. The skills you teach to students are the basis for this respect. If everyone learns to respect each other, a positive atmosphere for learning can be created.

7. Collaboration with families. "The first and primary educators of children are their parents." (The Religious Dimension of Education in a Catholic School, 43) This should encourage "a strong partnership between a Catholic school and the families of the students."

8. Leadership roles. "Love for and fidelity to the Church is the organizing principle and the source of strength of a Catholic school."

Religious communities are encouraged to persevere in "the fulfillment of an educational charism" and to draw from their own educational traditions. Lay teachers in Catholic schools have important roles as "concrete examples of the lay vocation" and can even establish and run schools, with the recognition of "competent ecclesiastical authority." Leaders in Catholic schools and church authorities must strive for "mutual esteem and reciprocal collaboration."

9. Creating a positive and supportive climate. "Some of the conditions for creating a positive and supportive climate are the following: that everyone agree with the educational goals and cooperate in achieving them; that interpersonal relationships be based on love and Christian freedom; that each individual, in daily life, be a witness to Gospel values; that every student be challenged to strive for the highest possible level of formation, both human and Christian. In addition, the climate must be one in which families are welcomed, the local Church is an active participant, and civil society – local, national, and international – is included. If all share a common faith, this can be an added advantage." (The Religious Dimension of Education in a Catholic School, 103). "Even students who are very young can sense whether the atmosphere in the school is pleasant or not. They are more willing to cooperate when they feel respected, trusted, and loved. And their willingness to cooperate will be reinforced by a school climate which is warm and friendly, when teachers are ready to help, and when they find it easy to get along with other students." (The Religious Dimension of Education in a Catholic School, 106)

Everyone directly involved in the school is a part of the community. While teachers, directors, administrators, and auxiliary staff are all important to this community, parents are the central figures. They are the most important and irreplaceable teachers in the education of their children. This community also includes the students, since they must be active in their own education. This community teaches children self-respect. This means that each child's needs and wants are sometimes subservient to family or community needs. This focus on looking "outside yourself" for one's development is important. As for teachers, the rest of this manual will clarify their role in this community as they create a well-managed classroom in their Catholic schools.

The Catholic school finds its true justification in the mission of the Church; it is based on an educational philosophy in which faith, culture, and life are brought into harmony. Through it, the local church evangelizes, educates, and contributes to the formation of a healthy and morally sound lifestyle among its members. The Holy Father affirms that "the need for the Catholic school becomes evidently clear when we consider what it contributes to the development of the mission of the people of God, the dialogue between the Church and the human community, to the safeguarding of freedom of conscience...." Above all, according to John Paul II, the Catholic school helps in achieving a double objective: "Of its nature, it guides men and women to human and Christian perfection, and at the same time helps them to become mature in their faith. For those who believe in Christ, these are two facets of the same reality."

CHAPTER ONE

Well-managed classrooms in a Catholic climate

Catholic education is an expression of the mission entrusted by Jesus to the Church He founded. Through education the Church seeks to prepare its members to proclaim the Good News and to translate this proclamation into action. Since the Christian vocation is a call to transform oneself and society with God's help, the educational efforts of the Church must encompass the twin purposes of personal sanctification and social reform in light of Christian values.

"To Teach as Jesus Did: A Pastoral Message on Catholic Education" (1972), by the National Conference of Catholic Bishops, in *The Catechetical Documents, A Parish Resource*, p. 88.

The concept of classroom management is broader than the notion of student discipline. It includes all the things teachers must do to foster student involvement and cooperation in classroom activities and to establish a productive work environment (Sanford, Emmer, & Clements, 1983).

The Second Vatican Council stated the issue this way: "The Catholic school pursues cultural goals and the natural development of youth to the same degree as any other school. What makes the Catholic school distinctive is the attempt to generate a community climate in the school that is permeated by the Gospel spirit of freedom and love. It tries to guide the adolescents in such a way that personality development goes hand in hand with the development of the 'new creature' that each one has become through baptism. It tries to relate all of human culture to the good news of salvation so that the light of faith will illumine everything that the students will gradually come to learn about the world, about life, and about the human person." (Declaration on Religious Education, 8)

So, a Catholic school has a community climate that is permeated by the Gospel spirit of freedom and love. All schools, secular or religious, should have as a goal human knowing, or knowledge. In a Catholic school, however, this human knowing should be illumined with the light of faith. So Catholic schools blend together the twin tasks of religious formation and human education for life in the world. This can be described as the religious dimension central to Catholic schools.

This does not mean that Catholic schools have all the answers. In fact, even though they have many answers, they have many more questions. These questions pertain to the most important issues in life:

- Why did God make me?

- Who am I?

- Who are you?

- What am I doing here?

- What are you doing here?

- Is the universe friendly?

- Does life have purpose?

- Does my life have purpose?

In the Catholic faith, the answers to these ultimate questions of life lie in the belief that one should trust in God as Creator and Father, as the Son who is Redeemer and Lord, as the Holy Spirit who is Sanctifier. But, there are still many more questions than answers, whether it be questions about history, geography, chemistry, math, or religion.

In order for children to gain control of their lives and realize a sense of academic and personal fulfillment, they must first learn how to accept responsibility for their behavior, how to respect the rights of others, how to solve problems, and how to make choices and decisions that can benefit them or that are in the best interest of others. Teachers in Catholic schools who maintain a well-managed classroom empower their students to attain these goals.

The Social Skills Curriculum that Boys Town teaches is particularly important in a Catholic school environment. It is one of the concrete means whereby there is created "a community climate in the school that is permeated by the Gospel spirit of freedom and love." From the simplest skill of following instructions to the more advanced skill of problem-solving, success in these areas helps us move toward true freedom and love.

▶ Positive classroom management

Until very recently, discussions about classroom management have placed too much emphasis on controlling unproductive student behavior and not enough emphasis on creating a learning environment that encourages productive student behavior. Discipline should not be limited to something you do after a student has done something wrong. Instead, discipline should restructure your relationship with your students to facilitate effective classroom management and, ultimately, to imbue them with a positive self-image and a sense of responsibility.

Frequently, the strategies teachers in private and public schools use in an attempt to effectively manage their classrooms and deter problems often contribute to problems, or make them worse. The most frustrating problems and unpleasant experiences associated with teaching are oftentimes the basic classroom management issues teachers face each and every day.

This book supplies a specific, detailed program that is designed to help you motivate and encourage your students to develop and maintain responsible behaviors that are essential to their success – both inside and outside the classroom.

Whether you are an experienced or a beginning teacher, this manual offers a comprehensive curriculum of social skills and systematic teaching techniques along with practical classroom management strategies.

Thorough reviews of classroom management done by some of the most prominent researchers in the field (Brophy, 1983; Doyle, 1986; Charles, 1989; Duke & Meckel, 1984; Wolfgang & Glickman, 1986; and Jones & Jones, 1990) suggest that five major factors can be correlated with effective classroom management:

1. A sound theoretical foundation and understanding of classroom management and the needs of students.

2. Strong, positive teacher-student and peer relationships.

3. Instructional methods that motivate students.

4. Organizational and group management techniques that maximize students' "on-task" behavior.

5. Problem-solving and behavior management techniques that empower students to assume responsibility for managing their own behavior.

If students are motivated to learn, if they feel good about the classroom environment and the relationship they have with you, if they can manage themselves and accept responsibility for their behavior, and if they feel empowered to improve, then and only then can you effectively teach and your students truly learn.

Effective classroom managers create classroom environments that are positive, supportive, and at the same time, well-structured. Effective classroom managers maintain structure in their classrooms through the effective use of management practices that help students acquire the necessary skills to think and problem-solve, accept responsibility with regard to rules, limits, and the needs of others, and develop a positive self-image.

For more than 80 years, Boys Town's mission has been to improve the way children are treated, regardless of their race, creed, or handicapping conditions. We are proud to expand this mission to include the goal of making the nation's schools a better place for all students.

▶ Boys Town's Education Model

"There are no bad boys. There are only bad environments, bad examples, bad thinking."

Father Edward J. Flanagan
Founder of Boys Town, 1917

When Father Flanagan said these words, sometimes all it took to help a homeless or wayward youth were love, compassion, and a place the child could call home. But as youth problems became more difficult and more complex, Boys Town realized the need to combine compassion with the competence that comes from dedicated professionals working in a healthy learning environment.

Boys Town's current programs have their origins in the efforts of professionals who designed, developed, and implemented the Teaching-Family Model (Phillips, 1968; Phillips, Phillips, Fixsen, & Wolf, 1974). From those origins, Boys Town has spent more than 20 years developing its own Teaching Model (Coughlin et al., 1983; Baron, Cunningham, Palma, & Phillips, 1984; Peter, 1986). Since the program's inception, Boys Town has devoted time, energy, resources, and personnel to disseminating its technology to programs serving troubled children and youth nationwide.

The Boys Town Education Model is a good example of this technology transfer – taking the basic techniques of its family-based Model and transferring them to a school setting as a powerful and innovative approach to positive and effective interventions for troubled students. A success-oriented program of personalized social skills instruction is the hallmark of the Boys Town Education Model. Initiated in 1977 at a residential school in Montana, the key concepts were brought to Boys Town in 1979 and further developed. These concepts are described in detail in this manual.

By implementing the Education Model in its classrooms, Boys Town has demonstrated that schools can significantly reduce discipline problems while directly and humanely teaching vital life skills in a positive school climate. Work by professionals at Boys Town and elsewhere (Larson, 1989; Czerwionka, 1987) has shown that difficult-to-teach, behaviorally disordered adolescents

can be effectively taught a variety of social skills. Two years after initiating its campus school program, Boys Town became actively involved in the nationwide dissemination of the Model. Today, public and private schools across the country implement the Boys Town Education Model with great success.

Part of the appeal of the Boys Town Education Model is that it is one of the few programs that can be integrated into the entire school day and across the curriculum. This helps to overcome some of the generalization problems associated with programs that occur only in one classroom or outside the school. Research evidence suggests that nonschool programs have little effect on school behavior (Jones & Offord, 1989).

Schools were made for children and learning. This simple premise underlies what we believe should be true about any good school program. It is our contention, therefore, that all students must experience success in school, be it academic, vocational, athletic, or artistic success. Whether the individual becomes a good math student or a poor math student, a good athlete or a poor athlete, is, in all probability, less dependent upon the student's academic and physical characteristics than upon the student's social/emotional skills (Cartledge & Milburn, 1978; Stephens, 1978; Hope & Cobb, 1973; Borich, 1971).

Unfortunately, many youth have not acquired the social behaviors necessary to effectively and appropriately interact with peers and adults in school settings. As a result, they do not achieve academic success. These students are the same youth who have not had other success experiences, and have been identified by school personnel as discipline problems, behaviorally impaired, emotionally disturbed, or being at-risk. Their problems are compounded by the fact that the very social behaviors they lack are the same ones employers have identified as being vital to success in the world of work (Gresham, 1981). There is hope. Researchers have found social skills training to be effective in developing job-related skills in learning-disabled and behavior-disordered adolescents (Montague, 1988).

The last decade has seen rapid growth in the number of youngsters identified as special-needs students and in the programs developed to serve them. Clearly, one of the program needs is social skills instruction. Hansen, St. Lawrence, and Christoff (1980) found conduct-disordered youth to have poorer social skills than "normal" youth. Less knowledge of social skills was found to be highly associated with a wide range of behavioral problems (Venziano & Venziano, 1988).

Present methods of teaching socialization to school-age children rely primarily on nonstructured or informal social experiences encountered in schools, at home, and in the community (Clark, Wood, & Northrop, 1980). The school is the only professionally staffed agency that sees virtually all children, making it an ideal avenue for teaching social skills. For approximately 180 days each year, the nation's schools provide youth from age 6 to 18 with a sizable portion of their nonstructured informal social experiences. It seems reasonable then to assume that our schools could provide a setting that emphasizes social behavior as a structured part of the school curriculum, beginning a process of helping students become more socially adept.

Developing a systematic means to routinely teach socialization to school-age

children poses quite a challenge. However, shifting the emphasis of instruction from a solely academic curriculum to a combination of academic and social behaviors does not entail lengthening the school day, eliminating required course work, or extending graduation requirements. Rather, it requires the dedication of school personnel in addressing social behavior as an ongoing part of the school curriculum in all classrooms, corridors, playgrounds, and office areas each and every day. Such dedication and vigilance in addressing social behavior obviously requires that teachers and administrators in Catholic schools be provided with sound theoretical principles and practical approaches to guide their teaching efforts. Education should not and cannot be for the select few who come from environments that help them become not only academically inclined, but also socially acceptable to peers and adults. Schools have group life, a vast range of possible activities, many caring adults, and a mandate to use these resources for the welfare of all children, including the troubled or troublesome child. Boys Town's goal has been, and continues to be, to develop an effective school program that promotes success through teaching social skills and building relationships, and serves as a model for others to use, benefiting youth nationwide. This program is the Boys Town Education Model.

▶ Components of the Boys Town Education Model

The Boys Town Education Model is firmly rooted in principles of applied behavior analysis and social learning theory. Its underlying premise is that behavior is learned through feedback on behavior and its environmental consequences (Bandura, 1969). The Model's focus is on teaching because troubled youth have social skills deficiencies and have not yet learned or been effectively taught how to interact with others in a socially appropriate way (Wolf, Phillips, & Fixsen, 1972; Sarason, 1968; Shah, 1966, 1968).

This behavioral model involves the identification of desirable prosocial behavioral expectations, the effective use of instructional strategies to teach those expectations, the application of an incentive system, and the effective implementation of reinforcement principles. The following elements have been developed and refined for use within a school context:

1. Social Skills Curriculum

2. Teaching Interactions

3. Motivation Systems

4. Administrative Intervention

The combined use of these program components provides educators with the technology to help all students – from those in the regular classroom to those in the most-restrictive special education environment – build social skills to maximize their personal effectiveness. The following section is a brief review of each of these four program components.

Social Skills Curriculum

The Boys Town Social Skills Curriculum for schools provides the foundation for a structured educational approach to the socialization of school-age children. The curriculum offers a manageable yet well-defined set of 16 social behaviors encompassing adult relations, peer relations, school rules, and classroom behaviors. This set of skills enables teachers to go beyond merely labeling problem behaviors (e.g., compulsive talker, lazy, restless, etc.), which often hinders identifying specific alternative behaviors that should be promoted, reinforced, strengthened, or taught. Here are the curriculum skills:

1. Following instructions

2. Accepting criticism or a consequence

3. Accepting "No" for an answer

4. Greeting others

5. Getting the teacher's attention

6. Making a request

7. Disagreeing appropriately

8. Giving criticism

9. Resisting peer pressure

10. Making an apology

11. Engaging in a conversation

12. Giving compliments

13. Accepting compliments

14. Volunteering

15. Reporting other youths' behavior

16. Introducing yourself

Teaching Interactions

While the social skills identify what to teach, the Teaching Interaction® guides how to teach, using specialized approaches similar to the direct instructional techniques advocated by Stephens (1978) and the structured role-play activities of Goldstein, Sprafkin, Gershaw, and Klein (1980). The greatest opportunity for skill generalization comes about through the instruction of skills in naturalistic settings, including classrooms, hallways, and offices (Gresham, 1982). Teaching Interactions promote this generalization.

Teaching Interactions differ from other social skill approaches by using a brief interactive instructional sequence with the student when the behavior occurs. This technique uniquely combines efforts to manage student behavior with the care and concern of teaching an alternative appropriate social behavior. Capitalizing on the teachable moment, when the learner is active and the learning is relevant, the Teaching Interaction allows the teacher to deal with behavior problems in an efficient, effective, and humane fashion (Downs, Kutsick, & Black, 1985; Phillips, Phillips, Fixsen, & Wolf, 1974).

Most educators find a smooth flow within the Teaching Interaction sequence. It can be used with any number of social behavior problems and can be applied in regular or special education settings. Teaching Interactions are concrete and provide positive instruction. Anyone who works with students (e.g., counselors, teachers, psychologists, administrators) can use the Teaching Interaction technique. Educators need only view the inappropriate behaviors of students as vital learning/teaching opportunities, not as personal insults or challenges to authority.

Motivation Systems

While the Boys Town Education Model uses Teaching Interactions to establish new behaviors, it also is essential for many troubled youth to earn and receive positive consequences when they use desired behaviors so that these newly acquired behaviors can be strengthened. This systematic applica-

tion of immediate consequences is part of what is known as the Motivation Systems. (Note: The Motivation Systems are used in special education or self-contained classrooms and may or may not be utilized within your school environment.)

Many students are motivated to learn without extrinsic rewards. For these youth, the combined use of clear behavioral expectations as defined by the Social Skills Curriculum and the instruction offered through a Teaching Interaction serve to develop highly successful student behavior. However, students with significant social skills deficits – students identified as behaviorally disordered, at risk, or emotionally disturbed – often lack motivation to learn and alter behavior. These students must be given help early on through external measures that hopefully will later lead to the development of an internal desire to learn (O'Leary & Drabman, 1971). The Motivation Systems provide a comprehensive framework for consistently applying principles of learning that will maximize behavior change for these students (Downs, Bastien, Brown, & Wells, 1987).

At the root of the Motivation Systems is a token economy. In the context of a Teaching Interaction, student behavior is confronted and the student earns negative consequences in the form of points. (When students use appropriate behaviors, they earn positive consequences, also in the form of points.) The immediacy of the consequences (points) helps motivate behavior change. Students accumulate positive points to gain access to reinforcers, including tangible items, privileges, and activities.

The Boys Town Motivation Systems are incorporated as a comprehensive framework that helps students with moderate-to-severe behavioral deficits add social skills to their repertoire of behaviors. The three-level token economy reflects stages of skill acquisition and provides the appropriate degree of structure and support that is necessary at each developmental level. This multi-level approach meets each student's individual needs while providing a gradual transition from artificial consequences to more naturally occurring forms of feedback and internal controls.

Administrative Intervention

Historically, schools often have viewed their role in discipline as one of providing punishment for rule-breaking behavior. This punishment frequently has included suspensions, expulsions, shortened school days, administrative transfers, and ignored truancies (Grosenick & Huntze, 1984). These forms of punishment have questionable effectiveness, are potentially harmful, often lead to a punitive school climate, and may, in some cases, violate statutes protecting the rights of handicapped youth.

Administrative Intervention® allows school administrators to function as effective change agents in response to more serious or continuing school discipline problems. It extends the teaching focus found in the other components of the Boys Town Education Model to include working with students who have lost self-control and been sent to the office. This approach, which includes Teaching Interactions and behavioral rehearsal (practice) adapted from the Boys Town Teaching Model, assumes that discipline is a process of training for correction or teaching alternative ways of responding to stressful classroom or school situations.

Deficits in social behavior (e.g., following instructions, accepting criticism, accepting "No" for an answer, resisting peer pressure) often make it difficult for students to remain in the classroom and, eventually, even in the school program (Schumaker, Hazel, Sherman, & Sheldon, 1982). The Boys Town Social Skills Curriculum (Brown, Black, & Downs, 1984) and a set of procedures designed to help administrators remain calm provide the framework for helping students regain self-control, then teaching them vital social skills and school expectations. An established sequence of consequences for office referrals promotes consistency and predictability while allowing for individualization of responses to rule violations. The goal of this teaching procedure, unlike many discipline policies aimed at the student's exclusion from school, is the youth's successful return to the classroom.

The procedures encompassed within the administrative format are used by administrators or designated persons (e.g., guidance counselors, psychologists, behavior interventionists) across the country. While Administrative Intervention is often used independently of other Model components, it provides crucial support when Motivation Systems are used within a school program.

▶ Summary

All schools, secular or religious, should have as a goal, human knowing, or knowledge. In a Catholic school, however, a climate must be created for students where this knowledge is illuminated by the light of faith. So Catholic schools blend together the twin tasks of religious foundation and human education for life in the world. This can be called the religious dimension that is central to Catholic schools.

In order for children to gain control of their lives and achieve religious and academic fulfillment, they must first learn a number of skills: accepting responsibility for their behavior; respecting the rights of others; solving problems; and making choices that can benefit them or are in the best interest of others. Teachers in Catholic schools who create and maintain well-managed classrooms empower their students to reach these goals.

The Boys Town Education Model is a comprehensive, systematic method of teaching prosocial skills to youth. Its four components – the Social Skills Curriculum, Teaching Interactions, Motivation Systems, and Administrative Intervention – help students learn productive ways of managing their own behavior and interacting with others. It combines the best of skill-based teaching with care and concern, resulting in improvements in students' behavior, self-esteem, and relationships with others.

While this manual contains some of the reading material used in training educators and provides an overview of the technical components of the Boys Town Education Model (both of which are vitally important to the proper training of education staff), the reader is cautioned not to view this manual as the sum and substance of the Model. These materials alone do not enable someone to fully understand and implement the Boys Town Education Model. For its own schoolteachers and the staff members of schools that contract with Boys Town, Boys Town provides three to five days of intensive skill-based training on the implementation of

the Model's components. The training process includes lectures, videotapes, and behavioral rehearsals that have proven effective in the development of trainees' skills. Furthermore, Boys Town has found that training, combined with ongoing consultation from individuals with experience in the Boys Town Education Model and systematic evaluation input, form the foundation for a successful education program and effective classroom management.

Student rights

Historically, children's rights have gone unrecognized. Not until the latter part of this century has this begun to change.

Children are neither an influential lobbying group nor do they have societal power that allows them to advocate for themselves. Because youth spend the majority of their time in school, educators are the advocates responsible for making school a safe and productive environment. Boys Town is committed to this goal and strives to provide a safe haven for each and every child served. This environment not only is free from abuse, but is one where children can grow spiritually, emotionally, intellectually, and physically. It is a place that respects the rights of a child and employs the most positive and least restrictive practices in educating children. Boys Town's mandate is: "As much freedom as possible, as little restriction as necessary."

▶ Promoting safe environments

The Boys Town approach to promoting safe environments has multiple components. These are:

1. Policies and procedures

2. Training in positive interaction styles

3. Ongoing program evaluation

4. Regular student interviews

5. Staff Practice Inquiries

6. Training in the rights of children

All of these components are integrated into the education systems with the major emphasis on the provision of safe, humane care. Information from these various components is constantly used to update and modify the school program when necessary.

Policies and procedures

The commitment of Boys Town Schools to provide safe environments begins (but does not end) here. Each staff member is made aware of written policies and procedures that relate to protecting the rights of children. These not only emphasize the intent of the education program but also contain the procedures followed when potential policy violations occur. Policies and procedures set in motion other specific components.

Training in positive interaction styles

All staff members are trained in positive techniques for interacting with or helping children change their behavior while respecting their basic dignity, differences, and freedom. (See Chapter 11: "The Teaching Interaction.") Also, all educators are trained to promote positive relationships with each child. (See Chapter 3: "Building and Maintaining Relationships.")

Ongoing program evaluation

Educators are provided with systematic feedback on teaching effectiveness through regular evaluation reports. These reports give all staff insight into the quality of education provided for children. Routine updates on school attendance, academic progress, and behaviors are a valuable method of monitoring overall program quality. One of the features of a humane school is the extent to which it succeeds in reaching the goals for which it was established. Routine reporting of progress on important goals helps a school achieve its goals.

Regular student interviews

Interviews are conducted routinely in the teacher evaluation process. During these interviews, each student is asked whether he or she has experienced any mistreatment by staff or others. Each child also is asked to express his or her opinion about the pleasantness and supportiveness of teachers and administrators. These questions provide important information regarding the school atmosphere. The emphasis here is on how goals are reached and the methods that are used. Information derived from these questions can be used to improve staff interaction and communication skills.

Staff Practice Inquiries

Any questionable staff practice is followed up by a Staff Practice Inquiry. Staff Practice Inquiries are investigations into situations where the use of inappropriate practices is suspected. These investigations usually result from information contained in a youth report or a consumer report, or from observation by staff.

All allegations obtained from any source about less-than-optimal care are investigated thoroughly and promptly. The fact that Boys Town promptly initiates Staff Practice Inquiries makes it clear that Boys Town takes its protective role seriously. The Boys Town practice is to investigate all claims regardless of their perceived validity or their perceived seriousness. Even relatively benign allegations are investigated in order to sensitize all staff members to the importance of maintaining high-quality standards.

It is the collective responsibility of all educators to safeguard the rights of children. Any suspected abuse observed by children, staff, or others should be reported immediately, as mandated by law. When such a report is received, the administration immediately initiates a Staff Practice Inquiry. The child and adult allegedly involved are interviewed along with others who may have relevant information. The facts are established and conclusions reached as quickly as possible. Quick action is important so that any danger or discomfort experienced by a child can be eliminated or so that any harm to an innocent staff member's reputation can be minimized.

Confidentiality is maintained to the greatest degree possible in all Staff Practice Inquiries. Total anonymity can often be maintained. Sometimes, anonymity cannot be guaranteed when a child may be at some risk, mainly because relevant persons need some information during the course of the inquiry process. For instance, parents or legal guardians are immediately informed of any allegation. In cases where serious allegations are made, Child Protective Services agencies are informed so that they can decide whether to conduct their own investigation.

Another important phase of Staff Practice Inquiries is the debriefing phase. Verbal and/or written reports are given to persons who have the right to know about any outcomes. It is important that relevant persons are kept informed, not only to protect the interests of the child but also to protect the reputation of innocent staff members who are involved.

Training in the rights of children

All Boys Town educators who work with children receive training to increase their sensitivity to the rights of children. Typically, this training occurs before educators work with children. Subsequent to training, educators are updated through materials and meetings provided by their administration. Educators are provided with rules about what to do or not to do in specific situations, as well as guidelines that augment the sound judgment required of any person involved in educating students.

The rules and guidelines used at Boys Town are outlined in this chapter. These are not inclusive but give a good overview of the training content. Legal precedent is noted where appropriate.

▶ Boys Town student rights

The goal of a good education program should be to teach children to make good choices and to become self-reliant. Boys Town bases its student rights on this premise; some are further supported by legal precedent. Our student rights are:

1. Right to privacy

2. Right to one's own possessions

Teachers should not conduct routine secret searches of a student's desk, locker, or person. Searches should be in the interest of a child's well-being and should be conducted by an administrator.

Students' right to privacy was challenged under the 4th Amendment by New Jersey vs. TLO (469 US 325, 1985). The United States Supreme Court determined that schools do not act *in loco parentis* and are governed by search and seizure laws. Schools, however, need only have probable cause, rather than reasonable suspicion which law enforcement authorities must have, in order to conduct a search. Student lockers and desks are possessions of both the school and the student during the school year. Although school administrators have the right to search these, this right should be clearly stated in school policy. Children's school records should be released only with the written permission of a child's parent or legal guardian.

It is important to note that students do not waive the right to privacy when bringing personal possessions on to school grounds. However, teachers should help ensure that no student possesses dangerous items (drugs, weapons, etc.) by notifying administrators if they suspect that a student has such items at school. Administrators have the right to confiscate dangerous possessions and turn them over to law enforcement.

Teachers also should see that each student has the necessary school supplies. If a student does not have supplies, the items should be provided by the school and further replacement items purchased by the student .

Teachers may exercise reasonable control over the personal possessions a student brings to class by instructing that the items be turned over to the teacher. The student also could opt to put the items away and take them home at the end of the school day. If a teacher limits or restricts a student's use of a personal item, the student should be told how to earn back the use of the item.

3. Right to freedom of movement

In Boys Town schools, restrictions on break time or recess only occur in response to immediate discipline concerns. These restrictions should not be used routinely or for extended periods of time. Teachers should use time-out very judiciously. Time-out is generally best suited for young children. It involves removing a student from a reinforcing event, not from an aversive event. The key to its appropriate use is to ensure that "time-in" is employed; the classroom must first be a reinforcing environment for the student.

4. Right not to be given meaningless work

Homework, additional work, or meaningless assignments are not given as a punishment to students in Boys Town schools. Assigned work is designed to promote academic progress.

5. Right to access file material (The Family Educational Rights and Privacy Act, 1974)

School records are made available to students with permission from their parents or legal guardians. Students cannot be forced to sign statements agreeing with behavior plans or school reports. They can, however, sign statements indicating they have read the materials. Students have a right to disagree with information in their file and may sign a formalized statement to that effect. Student files should be treated as confidential.

6. Right to nourishment

Teachers in Boys Town schools may not make lunch contingent on behavior, or ask that a less adequate lunch be served as a behavioral consequence. Access to water cannot be denied, but teachers can set reasonable periods of time for students to obtain drinks.

7. Right to communicate with signifi-cant others (6th Amendment)

Students have the right to contact their families and to see school support personnel (administrators, counselors, etc.). School personnel may set times when services are available. Although teachers may not deny students the right to communicate, they may exercise reasonable control over the timing and form of the communication.

8. Right to treatment

Teachers should assist each student's progress toward educational goals. They should set and maintain both academic and behavioral expectations, adjusting Individual Education Plans (IEP) when needed to ensure success. Special education students must have an IEP and may not be denied an education (Public Law 94-142).

9. Right to interact with others

Extended periods of physical isolation should not be used as a punishment. Separation of the student from the instructional group should be used only for short periods to promote appropriate behavior and academic learning. Teachers should not instruct students to isolate another student as a punishment. Students may, however, be prompted to ignore peer problems.

10. Right to respect of body and person

Physical restraint should be used only as a last resort to prevent a student from harming himself or others. Sarcasm, name-calling, labeling, and any other humiliating verbal statements directed toward a student must be avoided. Corporal punishment also must be avoided as a disciplinary action. It is not subject to the 8th Amendment; most states have no laws regulating its use. In the case of Baker vs. Owen (423 US 907, 1975), the Supreme Court decided that corporal punishment could be used without prior parental approval under the following guidelines: 1) it not be used as the first line of punishment, and 2) school officials need to be present to serve as witnesses. Boys Town strongly believes that schools should use positive methods to teach prosocial behaviors. Suppressing behavior through coercive means has only a temporary effect; aversive discipline methods generate counteraggression.

11. Right to natural elements

Teachers should not routinely restrict a student from outdoor activities, except in response to immediate behavioral concerns. Although they can use loss of recess as a behavioral consequence, teachers should not restrict access to recess for extended periods of time.

12. Right to freedom of expression (1st Amendment)

Administrators can regulate freedom of expression associated with curriculum and school activities. They can censor individual expression if it disrupts the educational process or puts the rights or safety of others in jeopardy (Tinker vs. Des Moines, 393 US 503, 1969; Bethel vs. Fraser, 478 US 675, 1986; Hazelwool vs. Kuhlmeier, 484 US 260, 1988).

▶ Education for All Handicapped Children Act (EHCA)

In 1977, Public Law 94-142 established rights for all handicapped children.

They have a right to a free, appropriate education at public expense that meets state educational standards. This education is provided under an Individualized Education Plan that is developed to meet the needs of the student, not the school district (Federal Register, August 23, 1977). The United States Supreme Court decided in the Board of Education vs. Rowley (458 US 176) in 1982 that the level of services must maximize the potential of the disabled child equal to the opportunities of nondisabled students. Further, the least restrictive environment must be provided to the maximum extent appropriate. Handicapped students also have a right to related supportive services that may be required. These include, but are not limited to, transportation, recreation, health, psychological services or counseling, and speech and hearing services.

Students under EHCA also have a right to due process, including the inspection of records and reports, prior notice, independent education evaluations, impartial hearings, and the right to appeal the hearing outcome. Students have a right to surrogate parent representation in the educational programming process, which is especially critical for students in residential placement.

Handicapped students have a right to not be expelled for behavior related to their exceptionality. In Honig vs. Doe (484 US 305, 1988), the Supreme Court determined that special education students cannot be expelled from school programming for more than 10 days, even if they are considered a threat to themselves or others. Suspensions require prior approval, but students may be suspended for up to 10 days without it being considered a change of placement. If a student's suspension exceeds 10 days, the multidisciplinary team must convene to change the child's IEP. For students in the regular education program, minimal procedures are needed for suspensions under 10 days.

More due process is needed for longer suspensions, with most states requiring students to be represented by counsel (Goss vs. Lopez, 419 US 565, 1975). Currently, U.S. courts are strongly debating the rights of students infected with the AIDS virus to attend school and receive protection under the 14th Amendment and the Rehabilitation Act, Section 504. Though courts have determined that students with AIDS are protected by the Rehabilitation Act, much controversy still surrounds these students attending classes. Individual districts should consult their governing laws.

▶ Convention on Rights of the Child

In order for schools to be an environments that foster self-reliance and self-confidence in our future generations, educators must treat students with the dignity and respect that should be afforded any human being. Successful education programs nurture students and encourage belonging, while recognizing that differences make individuals unique. The empowerment and protection of children as a universal agenda is ever increasing. To that end, the United Nations has become a powerful advocacy group in recognizing the rights of children everywhere.

On November 20, 1989, the general assembly of the United Nations created the *Convention on Rights of the Child*. It contains 54 articles; three specifically pertain to education and many affect schools. Because of its importance, all school personnel should read it. The three articles specifically related to education are summarized here:

Article 23 states that disabled children have the right to care, education, and training that will help them enjoy a full life and achieve the greatest degree of self-reliance and social integration possible.

Article 28 provides that children have a right to a free and compulsory education and that school discipline should be consistent with children's rights and dignity.

Article 29 states that children have a right to an education that develops their personalities, talents, and mental and physical abilities. Education should prepare a child for adult life in a free society. It should foster respect for parents, cultural identity, language, and values, as well as promote respect for others.

▶ Summary

Boys Town is concerned about protecting and assuring the free exercise of all rights and privileges of its students. The guidelines and processes described in this chapter provide evidence of this concern. However, success in assuring students' rights is not guaranteed by procedures alone, but comes from the "sense of quality" that is imbued in each educator. Each person should understand that it is his or her competence in developing and carrying out education plans, and diligence in monitoring personal actions and the actions of others that makes the real difference. Rules, guidelines, and procedures are necessary, but it is the commitment to providing the highest quality care possible that affords all students a safe environment in which to maximize their full potential.

CHAPTER THREE

Building and maintaining relationships

Justification from sin and God's indwelling in the soul are a grace. When we say a sinner is justified by God, is given life by the Holy Spirit, possesses in himself Christ's life, or has grace, we are using expressions which in different words mean one and the same thing, namely dying to sin, becoming partakers of the divinity of the Son through the Spirit of adoption, and entering into an intimate community with the Most Holy Trinity.

"General Catachetical Directory" (1971), approved by Pope Paul VI (March 18, 1971), in *The Catechetical Documents, A Parish Resource*, pp. 40-41.

Children spend nearly 13,000 hours in school between the ages of 6 and 18 and the majority of those hours are spent with a teacher inside a classroom. The quality of teacher-student relationships significantly affects whether students' needs are met.

When students' needs are being met in the classroom, they tend to behave more appropriately and learn more effectively (Jones & Jones, 1990).

The necessity for presenting a chapter on building and maintaining positive teacher-student relationships and creating positive and supportive classroom environments is based on the unfortunate reality that all too often, our classroom environments fail to meet students' basic personal and psychological needs. This is not to say that teachers in Catholic schools knowingly or willfully ignore these very critical needs, but rather points out how recommendations like, "Be tough," "Be clever," "Don't smile until the second quarter," or "Keep them busy and look like you're in charge" – once presented as simple prescriptions for effectively managing a classroom – have affected our school environments and classroom climates and are still exercised in many educational settings.

Teachers' relationships with their students often tend to be directed toward establishing control and fostering compliance rather than focusing on creating a classroom climate that represents an effective blend of warmth, care, and compassion with an appropriate amount of firmness, realistic tolerances, and competent teaching (Shores, Gunter, & Jack, 1993; Steinberg, 1992; Nichols, 1992; Steinberg & Knitzer, 1992).

"Many of the students will attend a Catholic school – often the same school – from the time they are very young children until they are nearly adults. It is only natural that they should come to think of the school as an extension of their own homes, and therefore a 'school-home' ought to have some of the amenities which can create a pleasant and happy family atmosphere. When this is missing from the home, the school can often do a great deal to make up for it." (The Religious Dimension of Education in a Catholic School, 27)

This is true for all students, but is especially important with younger students who need the security and sense of belonging they may not feel at home.

"Considering the special age group teachers are working with, primary schools should try to create a community school climate that reproduces, as far as possible, the warm and intimate atmosphere of family life. Those responsible for these schools will, therefore, do everything they can to promote a common spirit of trust and spontaneity. In addition, they will take great care to promote close and constant collaboration with the parents of these pupils. An integration of school and home is an essential condition for the birth and development of all of the potential which these children manifest

in one or the other of these two situations – including their openness to religion with all that this implies." (The Religious Dimension of Education in a Catholic School, 45)

That is why Boys Town's skills are a main ingredient in creating a family atmosphere. The various skills promote pleasantness, sensitivity, and respect for each other. When teachers use Boys Town's methods to teach these skills, they are helping create a warm, caring family atmosphere.

As a teacher, you adopt and use specific verbal and nonverbal behaviors to elicit appropriate behavior from your students, to reinforce positive behavior as it occurs, and to intervene in negative situations. In so doing, the strategies you choose are going to be affected, positively or negatively, by the context in which they are used and the nature and quality of the relationship you have established with your students.

Again, the traditional emphasis on classroom control and the administrative or self-imposed pressures to concentrate on content and get through the curriculum have either minimized the importance of teacher-student relationships or have made it more difficult to understand what role the relationship element has in education.

As much of the research indicates, the effectiveness of your instructional interactions with your students, academic as well as social, is largely dependent on the relationships you develop and maintain with them.

Too many children enter our schools and classrooms excited, eager, and exhibiting a readiness to learn only to later leave feeling disliked and unsuccessful (Morse, 1964; Cormany, 1975; Mortimore & Sammons, 1987; Purkey & Novak, 1984) and, in many instances, having failed academically as well as socially. The traditional emphasis on content and control may make it difficult for educators to see that relationships are important to learning, or more specifically, to agree that relationships significantly influence a child's educational experience. Current research indicates that teachers can and do make a difference in many students' lives even when facing the many societal factors that make the job of a classroom teacher more challenging and difficult. Teachers increase their effectiveness when they are provided with information about skills associated with effective teaching and when they receive feedback on how their behavior matches criteria for effective teaching (Jones & Jones, 1990). This chapter discusses the benefits resulting from strong teacher-student relationships and how to facilitate student learning and personal empowerment, and inspire a positive self-concept.

▶ Benefits of building strong teacher-student relationships

Teaching is an interactive process. The more positive your interactions are with your students, the more assured you can be that your interactions will be effective and mutually reinforcing. How students perceive themselves as learners and unique individuals, how much responsibility they assume for their behavior, and how well they learn and perform academically are affected significantly by what occurs at school and in your classroom. Individuals learn more effectively in environments that meet their basic personal and psychological needs (Jones & Jones, 1990). As a teacher in a Catholic school, you control many of the variables affecting your students' needs, which influence their academic achievement as well as their behavior. The nature and quality of the relationships you establish and maintain with your students form the basis of the climate in your classroom. And, a supportive and positive classroom climate creates an instructional environment that not only meets students' basic needs but also motivates them to demonstrate initiative, take risks, and commit themselves to learning. Strong relationships with your students contribute substantially to your ability to help promote growth and change in every student.

In addition to providing strong evidence that academic achievement and student behavior are influenced by the quality of the teacher-student relationship and that positive teacher-student relationships are associated with more positive student responses to school (Aspy & Roebuck, 1977; Norman & Harris, 1981), a significant body of research also indicates that students prefer teachers who display warm and friendly behavior toward them (Rosenshine, 1970; Norman & Harris, 1981). As Robert Bush (1954) noted in *The Teacher-Pupil Relationships*, "Teachers retain their effectiveness as professional persons only so long as they remain warmly human, sensitive to the personal needs of children, and skillful in establishing effective relationships."

The above findings also highlight the importance of modeling theory and its influence on the quality of the teacher-student relationship. Children learn not only by doing, but also by watching others. Much of a child's learning occurs by observing and subsequently modeling the behavior of the adults in his or her life. Research by Bandura (1969, 1977) indicates that individuals tend to emulate behavior of significant others – individuals who they perceive as competent, trusting, and who provide a major source of support, direction, and reinforcement. Teachers not only embody these qualities, but also are in an excellent position, second only to that of the child's family, to serve as role models for their students. When students have positive feelings about their school and their teachers, they are more likely to identify with and accept them as important role models. Furthermore, kids tend to model behavior if they think adults benefit by performing these behaviors (Jones & Jones, 1990), and they also are more likely to model behavior exhibited by several adults (Bronfenbrenner, 1970). These variables illustrate how important it is for you, as well as your colleagues throughout the school, to engage in skills and behaviors that create and maintain a positive and supportive environment for the students. Not only do positive relationships increase the effectiveness of your role-modeling, but your students' receptivity to more direct teaching also improves. Students will be more likely to accept your feedback, whether it takes the form of a compliment, praise or recognition for effort, an instruction to redo an assignment, or a Teaching Interaction to correct a socially inappropriate behavior. (See Chapter 11, "The Teaching Interaction.")

While it is true that positive teacher-student relationships will enhance the opportunity for all students to achieve a greater degree of academic and social competence, such relationships become even more critical for those students who enter your classroom with many unmet needs and a variety of behaviors that interfere with their social-emotional development and academic achievement. By improving the quality of your interactions with students, you can significantly increase the amount of productive

student behavior (Jones & Jones, 1990). Developing positive relationships with your students, however, will clearly not resolve all classroom problems nor prevent issues from occurring. Again, your concern, caring, and understanding must be delicately balanced with realistic limits, clear and specific expectations, and competent teaching.

▶ How relationships develop

Relationships do not develop over the course of a few days, weeks, or even months. Nor can a relationship ever be considered to be "developed." Rather, a relationship can be viewed as continually developing over time and across events and issues that arise as you interact with your students. Two key variables that significantly influence how relationships with your students evolve over time are, 1) the personal or affective quality of the relationship, and 2) how you communicate or relate to your students.

Generally speaking, there is a common set of behaviors and attitudes that are both socially acceptable and generally valued by members of our society. These behaviors and values include such concepts as honesty, sensitivity, concern and respect for others, a sense of humor, reliability, willingness to listen, and so on. Many students enter our schools and classrooms not yet having developed such values and behaviors because of poor role models, or damaged learning histories, or simply because they have not had the benefit of someone to guide them through a particular phase of development. As with so many other life skills, it becomes the school's responsibility – your responsibility – to teach students the skills needed to develop positive adult and peer relationships. While continuing to focus on the teaching of these critical skills, you also must maintain a high rate of positive interactions with your students, create opportunities during the school day when they can engage in open, personal discussions with you, and demonstrate a genuine interest in their activities.

Using quality components

While the components of Teaching Interactions (Chapter 11) and Effective Praise® (Chapter 9) can build relationships, one could use such "procedural" components and still not build relationships. Such teaching procedures must be accompanied by quality components and effective communication skills. Quality components are the positive verbal and nonverbal behaviors that accompany the procedural components. Such quality components include looking at the student, answering his or her questions pleasantly and enthusiastically, having a pleasant facial expression, smiling and using humor when appropriate, expressing concern and empathy, displaying appropriate physical contact such as a hug, a pat on the shoulder, a "high five," and so on.

The importance of using effective communication skills to enhance teacher-student relationships cannot be overemphasized. Warm, caring, open interpersonal interactions are critical in meeting many of your students' individual needs, from the most basic needs such as security and safety to the need to belong, to feel that they are unique, and to develop self-esteem.

"When students feel loved, they will love in return. Their questioning, their trust, their critical observations and suggestions for improvement in the classroom and the school milieu will enrich the teachers and also help to facilitate a shared commitment to the formation process." (The Religious Dimension of Education in a Catholic School, 110).

Maintaining a high ratio of positive to negative statements

Children of all ages are sensitive to praise and criticism from adults. Unfortunately, many adults – teachers in Catholic schools included – tend to notice disruptive or inappropriate behavior more often than they notice or comment on positive behavior. Research indicates that frequent negative remarks by teachers are usually accompanied by a student's dislike for school. Also, while we tend to believe that criticism will improve a student's behavior, research in fact suggests that the opposite is true. For example, in one class, students' off-task behavior increased from 8.7 percent to 25.5 percent when the teacher withdrew praise for on-task behavior. Concurrently, when the same teacher was asked to increase his criticism of off-task behavior; off-task behavior increased from between 31.2 to 50 percent (Becker, Engelmann, & Thomas, 1975).

Unfortunately, negative interactions not only have a negative effect on students' self-concept, but also contribute to a generally negative and unpleasant classroom environment, one in which the teacher is actually responsible for the increase in disruptive student behavior.

A more detailed explanation of the usefulness of providing students with positive feedback as well as an effective process for doing so is included in Chapter 9, "Effective Praise."

▶ Other elements of a positive relationship

As with any relationship, it is important to have shared experiences and "remember when" times to further enhance strong teacher-student relationships. One important way you can show interest and concern for your students is by taking the time to attend activities in which they are involved, both in and out of school. These might include sports, drama activities, dance recitals, scouting events, and so on. Evidence indicates that attending students' activities is often associated with dramatic improvement of those students (Jones & Jones, 1990).

Eating lunch with students or participating in playground activities also are excellent ways for you to show that you are "human" and that you do like to have fun. This participation not only affords an excellent opportunity to strengthen positive relationships, but also provides a natural setting in which you can model and teach cooperation, sportsmanship, and appropriate playground behavior.

Introducing yourself and welcoming the class through letters or notes sent to students prior to the beginning of the school year or semester also helps build and strengthen relationships. So does giving notes at other appropriate times, such as when a student has accomplished a particularly difficult task, shown significant behavioral improvement, or reached a goal. Greeting students individually at the door each morning or prior to the beginning of the period and offering some kind of positive statement also lets them know you care and that you're concerned about them. You also can demonstrate your interest in your students, as well as enjoy a good time with them, by participating in school activities such as "hat day," "casual dress day," carnivals, and other special events sponsored by the student council, various clubs, or other student groups.

Finally, relationship development also is an important part of dealing with problem behavior. As noted earlier in this chapter, the use of effective communication skills and quality components when using Teaching Interactions and Effective Praise contributes significantly to positive relationships. Furthermore, even when addressing negative behavior or a student's loss of self-control, you should use large amounts of empathy and praise to maintain and continue to develop positive relationships with students during these difficult times.

▶ Summary

Building strong relationships with your students is one of the more important aspects of the Boys Town Education Model. This is because having strong relationships with your students allows you to accomplish so many other goals. Relationships contribute much to the overall effectiveness of your teaching. Students cannot reach their full potential in school unless you and the other adults in your school encourage and invite them to do so.

"There are many ways to encourage students to become active participants in their own formation. Those with sufficient knowledge and maturity can be asked to help in the development of educational goals. While they are clearly not yet able to determine the final objective, they can help in determining the concrete means which will help to attain this objective. When students are trusted and given responsibility, when they are invited to contribute their own ideas and efforts for the common good, their gratitude rules out indifference and inertia. The more that students can be helped to realize that a school and all its activities have only one purpose – to help them in their growth toward maturity – the more those students will be willing to become actively involved." (The Religious Dimension of Education in a Catholic School, 106)

CHAPTER FOUR

Problem-solving

During recess, two fifth-graders are chosen to be on the same kickball team; both want to pitch and they begin to argue. On the way to fourth-period PE class, several students approach another student and ask him to skip class with them; the student doesn't want to, but he also doesn't want to lose face with friends. Before school, one student asks a classmate to do a book report for her and offers to pay for it; the classmate would like to have the money but is afraid of getting caught. During lunch, two students observe an older student aggressively attempting to extort money from a new student; one of the observers wants to report the event, the other doesn't.

Problems like the ones described above are not unusual. Students face conflict, confusion, difficult choices, and a wide array of other problematic situations every day. And, like it or not, as teachers, administrators, counselors, and other school staff, you invest as much time throughout the school day assisting students with problem mediation and social adjustment as you do with advancing their academic progress. Schools provide a unique environment for fostering social adjustment and problem-solving skills in children, since so many of the social interactions and events that occur can be monitored and used as real-life teaching and learning opportunities.

Problem-solving is a lifetime skill, one that students can use in or out of school, now or 10 years from now. There is no question that problem-solving skills are valuable to one's development. It has been said that psychological health is related to a problem-solving sequence consisting of the abilities to recognize and admit a problem, reflect on problem solutions, make a decision, and take action (Kendall & Braswell, 1982). Furthermore, problem-solving ability might be among the factors that contribute to an individual's use of prosocial, rather than anti-social, behavior (Goldstein, 1988). Some research suggests that improved problem-solving skills among students can lead to improved classroom behavior (Spivack & Schure, 1974). Caldwell (cited in Spivack & Schure, 1974) found that as alternative thinking improved, disrespect, defiance, inattentiveness, withdrawal, and overreliance on others all decreased. Inadequate problem-solving skills generally result in a student relying on socially inappropriate and ineffective solutions to real-life problems, particularly solutions that are aggressive or coercive in nature. Students with behavior problems have difficulty perceiving as many options, or the same kinds of options or behavioral options, as others, and are more likely to demonstrate rigid thought patterns (Spivack & Schure, 1974).

Why do so many of our students lack the requisite skills needed to effectively solve problems? One of the most obvious reasons for this may be modeling. For example, if a student frequently has seen others use withdrawal and submissiveness to solve a problem, he is apt to use this option when bullied by a bigger student who is demanding money. A student who comes from an environment in which individuals settle disagreements and obtain what they want through arguing and fighting – even though she may realize these solutions are unacceptable – may perceive aggression as her only option when another student on her kickball team also wants to pitch. These examples may help point out why many students may persist in their inappropriate responses to problems by submitting or retaliating, or why they may not even be aware that a problem exists. These students need to be taught how to identify and/or solve problems.

If students have an operational process or plan they can use when they face a challenge in or out of school, they are more likely to successfully recognize and resolve problems. Problem-solving also can be used retrospectively to help students make better decisions in the future.

It also is important to note that there are situations and times when problem-solving may not be appropriate as the first level of intervention. These include situations when you are attempting to teach a new skill to an individual or to the entire class; in such situations, Preventive Teaching® (Chapter 10), not problem-solving, is the appropriate procedure. You also should not have a student use problem-solving when dealing with inappropriate behaviors such as skill deficiencies (e.g., not accepting criticism, not accepting "No" for an answer, etc.), rule violations, or inattentive ongoing behavior. Such student behaviors require the consistent, concerned use of Teaching Interactions (Chapter 11). At times, you may be tempted to help a student problem-solve when he or she loses self-control, especially when the student is passive, withdrawn, crying, or complaining about unfairness. (See Chapter 12, "Ongoing Behavior.") In such cases, it is important to stay focused, regain the student's attention and cooperation, and complete the various teaching agendas. Later, when the student is calm and has fully regained self-control, you may choose or the student may ask you to initiate a problem-solving session.

There are times when students face serious problems. In such cases, you probably will not, and should not, feel comfortable discussing the problem with the student alone, and should seek the assistance and support of the school counselor, psychologist, or another qualified professional in the community. These problems could include trying to work through the serious illness or death of a friend or family member, parents' separation or divorce, or loss of a boyfriend/girlfriend. A final example is suicide ideation, which in and of itself is so serious that it requires immediate contact for professional help, as outlined in your school district policies and procedures. In fact, anytime you feel uncomfortable with a situation a student has brought to you, contact a qualified school or professional person in the community who can assist the student.

▶ What is problem-solving?

Problem-solving can be defined as a behavioral process that offers a variety of potentially effective options for dealing with a problem, and increases the probability of selecting the most effective solutions from among the various options (D'Zurilla & Goldfried, 1971).

Most of the research on problem-solving describes a process which includes the following five stages or competencies: 1) problem identification or general orientation, 2) problem definition, 3) generation of alternatives, 4) evaluation of the solutions, and 5) decision-making (Spivack & Schure, 1974).

The Boys Town Education Model uses the **SODAS**® method, a revision of a counseling process developed by J.B. Roosa (1973), to teach students the general skill of problem-solving. **SODAS** is an acronym for the following steps:

S – Defining the problem **situation**.

O – Examining **options** available to deal with the problem.

D – Determining the **disadvantages** of each option.

A – Determining the **advantages** of each option.

S – Deciding on the **solution/simulation**.

This general framework for problem-solving has a great deal of utility and flexibility. You can use the process to conduct group problem-solving, discussions such as those that occur during a class conference, or peer mediation sessions. Students also can use the skill components to solve interpersonal conflicts, such as how to deal with being asked to skip school, or intrapersonal problems, such as when a student loses her homework or forgets her PE uniform.

Regardless of whether the problem involves the entire class or an individual student, or is **interpersonal** or **intrapersonal** in nature, the primary focus of your teaching should be on using the process and teaching the students how to effectively use the **SODAS** method.

Situation

The problem-solving process begins with you helping the student clearly define the situation or problem, assuming that the student is able to recognize that a problem exists. Not all students possess this skill and this may be where you need to start. A problem can be defined for students as a situation in which they need to do something to get what they want, but they don't know what to do or how to do it (Kaplan, 1991).

Before a student can be expected to engage in the skill of problem recognition, he or she must first be able to determine whether or not a problem exists. For example, you might present your students with pairs of situations like the following for discussion.

Situation #1:

"You get home from school and realize that you left your science book in your locker. You have a unit test the next day. Is this a problem? Why or why not?"

Situation #2:

"You get home from school on Tuesday and realize that you left your science book in your locker at school and you have a unit test on Friday. Is this a problem? Why or why not?"

When helping younger students to recognize instances and non-instances of problems, more concrete examples and specific teaching, such as the use of pictures paired with a direct instructional approach, is probably more appropriate. For example, you might show elementary students a picture of a child being bullied by older kids on the playground and say, "Here's a problem situation. Several older kids start picking on you during recess. You want them to stop doing this but you don't know what to do to get them to stop. Why is this a problem for you?"

Before moving on to having your students define the problem situation, it is critical that they are competent in recognizing problems.

Once students can determine whether a problem exists, they are ready to define the problem or situation. This skill component is extremely important; many stu-

dents who have difficulty problem-solving know a problem exists but don't define it correctly. Oftentimes, students tend to leave themselves out of the problem, or their description of the problem is very vague and emotional (e.g., "I hate math class," "None of the boys in my class like me," "My PE teacher isn't fair and he always picks on me.").

To help a student pinpoint the specific problem, you can use general clarifying questions or statements to help the student more clearly focus on the issues (e.g., "Why don't you explain that further?"). However, it frequently may be necessary to ask more direct, specific questions to help the student talk about his or her issues (e.g., "Why do you hate math class?" or "Why do you think your PE teacher is unfair and picks on you?").

While exploring the situation with the student, it is extremely important that you engage in supportive verbal and nonverbal behaviors that communicate empathy, concern, and encouragement. Without these relationship quality components, your questions may become more like an interrogation that could cause the student to withdraw.

As the student more clearly defines the situation, you need to summarize what the student is saying. Such a summarization is particularly important before any options are discussed. The summarization helps you assure that all the relevant information has been reviewed and that you accurately perceive the student's situation. If the summarization is inaccurate or incomplete, the student then has the opportunity to correct any misperceptions. This is especially important at this point since the remainder of the process is built around the defined situation. Without an accurate or clearly defined situation, it will be difficult to generate useful options and a viable solution.

Options

The ability to generate a list of alternatives or options is probably the single most important problem-solving skill. Knowing what to do in case of failure is one that can prevent or decrease a student's frustration level or the need to engage in withdrawn or impulsive behavior. Spivack and Schure (1974) consider this skill: 1) the most powerful prediction of maladaptive behavior; 2) the skill that is best enhanced through training; and 3) the one that, when fostered, seems to also result in the greatest improvement in student classroom behavior. Knowing how to pursue or select alternative options also may be all the encouragement a student needs to keep on trying and not give up (Kaplan, 1991).

Once the situation is clearly defined, you should help the student generate options in the form of potential solutions to the problem. It is important to have the student generate the option that might solve the problem. Remember that the goal is to have the student develop his or her ability to solve problems as well as arrive at a solution.

To help students generate options, specifically ask the student how he or she might solve the problem or deal with the situation (e.g., "Can you think of a way to handle that?" or "What do you think you can do about this?"). After the student suggests an option, you need to continue to solicit options (e.g., "Can you think of any other ideas?").

Initially, students may have difficulty generating options or generating more than one option. Also, the suggestions offered may not be very helpful or realistic. Whenever a student gives an option, it is very important that you remain nonjudgmental. You can remain nonjudgmental by commenting positively about the student's participation in the process (e.g., "Well good, you've come up with a second option. You're really trying to think this through."). You also can offer a neutral comment and a prompt for more options (e.g., "Okay, that's one option. Can you think of another one?").

Remaining nonjudgmental can be very difficult, especially when the student suggests an option that would only result in more problems for him or her (e.g., "I'll just have to punch him out."). You need to remember that your role at this point is just to get the student to generate options. In that sense, this phase of the process is like "brainstorming." The next phase of examining the advantages and disadvantages will allow you to help the student judge the "wisdom" of his or her suggested options.

During the option phase, you may give your suggestions as well. However, this should be done only after the student has given all of his or her ideas. You may want to phrase the option as a question (e.g., "How about talking to your math teacher after class?") so that the student feels involved in the process. Over time, students will be better able to generate options and will be more comfortable doing so.

Once students can generate three or four different options for every situation or problem, they should be considered competent at this skill. Children as young as four are considered capable of developing this skill (Spivack & Schure, 1974).

Disadvantages and advantages

Once students are capable of generating several options to a problem, they must learn how to evaluate or analyze the advantages and disadvantages of each option. Each option should be evaluated according to two basic criteria: 1) efficacy, i.e., "Will this solution help me achieve my goal without causing me any additional problems?", and 2) feasibility, i.e., "Will I be able to take the action outlined in my options?" (Kaplan, 1991).

Your role is to help the student think through the efficacy and feasibility of each option. In a sense, you are attempting to teach the student that there is a cause-and-effect relationship between his or her decisions and what happens to him or her. As in generating options, it is important to have the student think through the advantages and disadvantages, with you skillfully guiding that process. If the student has difficulty thinking through the advantages and disadvantages, you can help by asking more specific questions (e.g., "Well, what do you think would happen if you told your PE teacher off or just didn't go to that class anymore?").

There may be a number of advantages and disadvantages for any given option. Again, since the goal is to help the student learn to think, it also is important in this phase to solicit additional advantages and disadvantages (e.g., "Can you think of any other advantages; any other problems?").

During this process, it is important for you to remain nonjudgmental and not argue with a student about his or her perceptions of the advantages and disadvantages. This can be difficult when the student seems enthusiastic about the unrealistic advantages of an option (e.g., "Yeah, it'd be great to fight it out because then he'd leave me alone and everybody would think I was bad."). Rather than argue about an advantage, you can simply acknowledge the student's view (e.g., "Okay, so you think that an advantage would be...."). Later, you can guide the student's judgment during the discussion of the disadvantages (e.g., "What happens if you don't win?" or "Could you get hurt?" or "What will your boss do if he hears you've fought with another employee?").

If a student clearly does not see or cannot verbalize an important advantage or disadvantage, you should offer your viewpoint and allow the student to react.

After discussing the disadvantages and advantages for the options, you should summarize by reviewing each option and the associated advantages and disadvantages. This summary review further helps the student see the cause-and-effect relationships.

Solution/simulation

The last step in the **SODAS** process involves having the student select the solution and prepare to successfully implement it by conducting any necessary "simulations" or role-play sessions. As a result of examining advantages and disadvantages, the student typically selects a workable option. It may not always be the best option from your point of view, but it is more important that it is the student's option. The student is more likely to be committed to make an option work if he or she is truly comfortable with it and feels ownership for the choice.

After the student has selected an option, you should encourage and reassure the student that the solution can be successfully implemented. In making the student comfortable with the solution, you can answer any questions the student may have about how to successfully implement it.

Another important aspect of improving the student's chance of success is for you to set up a role-play or practice session. These role-play sessions should be as realistic as possible. Often, you will know the people the student will need to interact with when implementing the solution (e.g., parents, friend, employers, principals, other teachers). Because you know these individuals, you can simulate their behaviors. For example, if an employer is fairly abrupt and somewhat stern, you can best help the student by portraying the employer in that manner. The role-play can be made more realistic by presenting the student with several possible responses so that he or she will be more comfortable and more likely to succeed.

Remember to express confidence in the student's ability to implement the solution. However, don't promise that the solution will work. As the practice session ends, you should prompt the student to check back after trying to implement the solution. If the student succeeds in solving the problem, praise him or her for doing so and for going through the problem-solving session. If the solution is not workable, be very supportive and empathic. You and the student can then return to the **SODAS** format to find a more successful solution.

Learning to problem-solve is a complex task, but as mentioned earlier in this chapter, it is a lifetime skill and one that is critical to your students' eventual success. Because participating in the problem-solving process is so important, it would be reasonable to have students earn significant positive consequences for demonstrating this skill.

Since many students have "solved" their problems in inappropriate ways in the past (e.g., running away, becoming aggressive), it is important to positively reinforce a student who indicates he or she would like to discuss a problem (e.g., "I'm having a problem with my PE teacher" or "I'm having a problem at my job. Can you talk with me about it?").

The complete use of the **SODAS** format during a problem-solving session is very important in teaching rational problem-solving skills to your students. When using the **SODAS** process, it is critical that you remember to always engage in supportive verbal and nonverbal behaviors that communicate care, concern, and empathy. In addition, two important distinctions related to how you teach and guide your students in the problem-solving process need to be made at this point. First, students should be encouraged to generate their own options to their own problems rather than you always telling them what they should do or what you think is the best solution. Students need to take ownership of their behavior. When they begin to generate alternatives, they are more likely to learn that they do have a certain amount of control over what happens to them. They also are learning critical thinking skills. Second, the emphasis again must be on teaching the students the process or skill of how to problem-solve rather than judging the solution itself. Students must be allowed to make mistakes or poor decisions in the process of learning how to make the most effective or reasonably "correct" decision. However, if the safety of the student or others is a concern, then you will have to steer the student toward a different solution.

Aside from formal problem-solving sessions, there are many other types of formal and informal activities that facilitate modeling and direct teaching of the **SODAS** process. Informally, there will be opportunities for discussion that may be prompted by television programs or current events. As your students express their opinions and points of view, you will be confronted with ideal opportunities to encourage your students to think, to weigh options, and to discuss the possible ramifications of their views and values.

While your students may possess the skills necessary to solve problem situations they face, the fact that they have these skills in their behavioral repertoire is not a guarantee that they will use them when confronted with a problem. Following are several factors to keep in mind as you work with your students on the difficult skill of problem-solving.

1. Model problem-solving for your students. Whenever appropriate, you should use **SODAS** or other problem-solving strategies. Talk with your students about situations in which you are using or have used **SODAS** to work through a problem.

2. Take the time to provide specific teaching for your students in the **SODAS** process. Assess their skills on a regular basis and provide follow-up teaching as needed.

3. Look for every opportunity to praise your students for their spontaneous use of **SODAS** or other appropriate problem-solving strategies throughout the day.

4. Promote generalization by encouraging your students to use their problem-solving skills outside of the classroom and the school setting. Assign homework or provide opportunities to engage in other activities that require your students to use these skills with peers as well as adults.

▶ Summary

Students must be taught how to solve problems. Problem-solving is an invaluable skill that students will need to have and use both in and out of school for the rest of their lives. In fact, problem-solving is so critical to students' health and successful adjustment and social competence that it is probably one of the single most important learning experiences you can provide for your students, even more important than many other areas of the curriculum you are currently teaching.

In summary, problem-solving has two important goals – to help students arrive at sound solutions to their problems and to teach them how to solve their problems in a systematic, rational way. The **SODAS** process, coupled with important relationships variables (e.g., active listening, empathy, concern), can help you accomplish these goals. And, because such problem-solving sessions also promote and establish trust between you and the student, critical relationship-building also occurs.

CHAPTER FIVE

Principles of behavior

The Boys Town Education Model has its foundation in social learning theory. This chapter will define the major components of this theory in order to provide a perspective on how current behaviors of youth are maintained, how to identify behaviors that may need to be changed, and how to institute a behavior-change process with these youth.

In order to understand and effectively use this theory, one must look at various concepts of the word "learned." A commonly held concept is that if a particular behavior has been taught, then it should have been learned. In the Boys Town approach, a behavior is believed to be learned when it has been successfully demonstrated over time in appropriate settings. When children have problems with a math concept, teachers generally go back and analyze their teaching approach, change it, and reteach the math concept. However, when children have prob-

lems engaging in appropriate social skills for the classroom, teachers are generally not as willing to analyze their teaching approach to the problem. They may assume that the skills students do not know should have already been taught and therefore learned. The Boys Town approach encourages a reteaching process, without the assumptions of learning, until appropriate behaviors are successfully demonstrated over time.

▶ The ABC pattern (three-term contingency)

Behavior does not occur in a void. Events that precede a behavior and events that follow a behavior affect on the future occurrence of that behavior. To fully understand the behavior itself, one must know what happens in the environment prior to the behavior as well as what occurs afterwards. It is helpful for educators to think of the ABC, or three-term contingency, pattern:

A = Antecedents – the events or conditions present in the environment before a behavior occurs

B = Behavior – what is done or said by a person

C = Consequences – the results, outcomes, or effects of a behavior

Behavior always occurs as a part of a contingency. The universe, according to social learning theorists, is a determined orderly place in which events do not just randomly happen. They happen as a part of a relationship to other events. We call this relationship a contingency. Contingencies are responsible for our learning histories as the probability of the occurrence of behavior is determined by its history of consequences (Cooper, Heron, & Heward, 1987).

Antecedents

The situation or context in which behavior occurs qualifies as the antecedent to that behavior. These conditions or events can be simple or complex, recent or historical. When analyzing the antecedents of a behavior, pay particular attention to who was present, what activities were occurring, the time of day or season of the year, and the location or physical setting.

Each of these alone or in conjunction with one another can set the stage for particular behaviors to occur. The more you know about the history of a student, the greater your understanding of the previous learning that has occurred with that student. Learning history can play a role in the antecedents of current behavior.

While all the antecedents for a behavior may be complex, a more simple stimulus (or set of stimuli) often may immediately precede a behavior. A doorbell ringing immediately precedes someone standing to answer the door; a student's smiling face first thing in the morning sets the occasion for a greeting; a green light at an intersection precedes the continuance of pressure on the gas pedal in the car; a student arguing with a teacher after an instruction is given precedes the teacher's behavior of intervening and teaching how to follow an instruction.

Behavior

What is behavior? Behavior is anything a person does or says that can be directly or indirectly observed (i.e., seen, heard, felt, touched, or smelled) and measured. For example, a teacher can directly observe the behavior of writing numbers on a math assignment by watching a student work on the assignment or indirectly observe the same behavior by noting the results – in this case, by seeing a completed math worksheet.

Consequences

Consequences are environmental changes that occur after a behavior in a relatively immediate, temporal sequence that alters the probability of future occurrence of that behavior (Cooper, Heron, & Heward, 1987). Consequences take one of two forms:

1. A new stimulus is presented or added to the environment, such as a student earning free time on the computer following the completion of a class assignment.

2. An already present stimulus is terminated or removed from the environment, such as

a student losing the privilege of free time on the computer because he did not accept criticism from his teacher about staying on-task.

Consequences will either increase or decrease the future rate of a particular behavior. When consequences increase the likelihood of the behavior occurring again, this is called " reinforcement." When a consequence decreases the likelihood of that behavior occurring again, this is termed "punishment."

Consequences can be natural or applied. Natural consequences are the typical outcomes of a behavior without any intentional human intervention. For example, scrapes and bruises are the natural consequences of falling down on a cement sidewalk; falling backwards is a natural consequence of leaning back too far in a chair.

Applied consequences for behavior are outcomes that are purposefully arranged. In the Boys Town Education Model, applied consequences can take the form of privileges the students earn for engaging in appropriate classroom behavior or appropriate academic tasks. They also can take the form of privilege losses for not completing academic tasks to a set criteria, or for not engaging in appropriate classroom behavior.

▶ Using the ABC pattern

Understanding the ABC pattern can help educators clarify why a behavior occurs. More importantly, it will aid them in helping their students change their behaviors. Many students engage in classroom behaviors that, if generalized to settings outside the classroom, will isolate them from family, friends, school activities, and their community. Due to various circumstances at home, some of these students have no one other than their teachers to help them make the needed changes for success. Using the ABC pattern helps teachers promote change in positive, effective, and efficient ways.

Teachers can help students change their behavior by manipulating antecedents, consequences, or both. Frequently, we think changing the consequence will work, and then are sometimes surprised when we don't get the result we wanted. But there may be times when altering the antecedents is a more effective way to change behavior. An example might be a person who is having trouble getting out of bed in the morning and who keeps hitting the snooze button on the alarm instead of getting up. He could change the antecedent by moving the alarm clock to the other side of the room. This would make it more difficult for him to immediately go back to sleep because he would have to get up and walk across the room to hit the snooze button. Since he is already up, it may encourage him to stay awake. Another example of changing antecedents is how a teacher would prepare her students for a school pep rally. Behaviors that should occur during the pep rally can be rehearsed ahead of time and the most relevant behaviors can be pointed out and discussed. Cues and subtle signals that will prompt appropriate behavior at the rally can be explained to the students.

In each of these situations, the antecedent conditions have been altered to help achieve the desired behavioral change. We call this Preventive Teaching and will discuss this in greater detail later in the book.

Changing consequences also can be effective. Specific verbal praise can be given when a student appropriately gets your attention. A student can earn a positive consequence for following your instructions to begin an assignment. Likewise, a student may lose a privilege for arguing with you about completing an assignment. By changing the consequences, you can help change a student's behavior.

The Boys Town Education Model has many built-in uses of the ABC pattern. For difficult, unique, or recurring student problems, use the ABC pattern to analyze the problem behavior and come up with a solution to help the student change.

▶ Some principles of behavior

Principles of behavior are the fundamental laws concerning the nature of behavior. They specify the relationships between behavior, the circumstances that surround that behavior, and the resulting outcomes. These principles are critical for educators as they approach the complex task of helping students change their behavior by instituting a behavior-change procedure (Cooper, Heron, & Heward, 1987).

Educators can use the techniques of positive and negative reinforcement to increase behavior, and positive and negative punishment to decrease behavior. They can use the techniques of generalization and discrimination processes to teach appropriate behavior for many different social situations. They also can use extinction, shaping, and fading techniques to help the student learn to respond to naturally occurring environmental reinforcers. See Figure 1 for a chart of behavioral terms.

▶ Positive reinforcement

Positive reinforcement means providing consequences immediately after a behavior to increase the likelihood that the behavior will occur again in the future. If the behavior occurs more often or gets stronger, then it can be assumed that the behavior was "reinforced" by the consequences. Therefore, if a behavior increases, regardless of what the consequence was, it has been reinforced.

Positive reinforcement can occur with natural or applied consequences. An example of a natural consequence for positive reinforcement is the rewarding feeling a high school basketball player gets when he makes a free throw that wins the game. The crowd cheers and his teammates pat him on the back. The results of this public praise will motivate him to continue playing basketball at school. An example of an applied consequence is a teacher's promise to a student that finishing an assignment in 10 minutes will earn her 10 minutes of computer time. When the student finishes her assignment on time, she gets to use the computer. This will help motivate the student to complete other assignments in a timely fashion.

Positive reinforcement can help a student learn a new behavior or maintain appropriate behavior. Figure 1 reviews this concept.

Here are some conditions that determine the effectiveness of positive reinforcement:

1. Appropriateness of the reinforcer. Rewards need to be individualized to make sure they are, in fact, reinforcing for the student. To determine appropriate reinforcers, ask the student, observe the student during

Figure 1

Matrix of Behavioral Terms

	Pleasant/Positive stimulus or event	Unpleasant/Negative stimulus or event
Presenting or Applying	**Term used:** Positive Reinforcement **Behavioral result:** Acts to strengthen the response **Examples:** Hugs, praise, points, etc.	**Term used:** Punishment **Behavioral result:** Weakens or may terminate the response but is highly susceptible to side effects **Examples:** Reprimands, threats, corporal punishment, etc.
Withdrawing or Removing	**Term used:** Response Cost **Behavior result:** Weakens or terminates the response **Examples:** Loss of points, traffic tickets, time-out, etc.	**Term used:** Negative Reinforcement **Behavior result:** Acts to strengthen the response **Examples:** Turning off a noisy radio, doing something that stops a baby from crying in church, etc.

his or her free time, let the student try a variety of reinforcers without having to display a certain behavior, have the student pick from a preset menu, and just try out reinforcers and observe the results from using them.

2. Immediacy of the reinforcer. To maximize their effectiveness, reinforcers need to be given immediately after the behavior you want to see increase. The more time that passes between the occurrence of the behavior and the giving of the reinforcer, the less effective the reinforcer is in strengthening the behavior. For example, it is the immediate verbal praise that follows a correct answer that makes a student want to learn the material being taught. Points are such an effective reinforcer because they can be given immediately after a behavior.

3. Amount or size of the reinforcer. The size of the reinforcer should fit the behavior. The longer the behavior takes to perform, the newer the behavior is for a student, or the more difficult it is to perform, the larger the reward should be.

4. Reinforcement contingencies. If reinforcement is to be effective, the student must receive the reinforcer only after performing the target behavior. A contingency is an "if... then" statement; if you do the behavior, then you get the consequence. For instance, "If you remain in your seat until I finish the lecture, then you may go to the shelf and get your journal." Be sure to make positive consequences contingent upon positive behavior. You also must analyze negative behavior to determine whether the rewards you are giving are inadvertently reinforcing or strengthening that negative behavior.

5. Reinforcement deprivation and satiation. In order to maximize the effectiveness of a reinforcer, an individual must experience some level of deprivation prior to delivery of the reinforcer. If a child has been playing computer games for the last 20 minutes, adding more computer time as a reinforcer might not be effective because the child may have become "satiated" with computer time. The concept of satiation also refers to the use of reinforcers when they are most in demand by the students. An example might be use of a compact disc recording as a reinforcer for one week of homework completion. If the CD is Frank Sinatra's greatest hits instead of a popular rock group's latest work, it probably would not be in demand by the teenage student. Thus, the CD would not be considered an effective reinforcer for the homework completion. The effectiveness of positive consequences is maximized by using a variety of reinforcers and by using those that are most in demand by students at the moment.

6. Use of the Premack Principle. This is better known as "Grandma's Law" and is another way to fully utilize positive reinforcement. The Premack Principle states that access to high-frequency behavior is contingent upon the occurrence of low-frequency behavior; for example, telling a student, "You may go to recess as soon as you finish questions one through five at the end of the chapter." The concept behind this principle is that a high-frequency behavior (e.g., going to recess) can serve as a reinforcer for a low-frequency behavior (completing assigned schoolwork).

Schedules of reinforcement

Schedules of reinforcement simply refer to how often reinforcers are given to a student. There are two basic schedules of reinforcement for delivering reinforcers. One is a "continuous schedule," where a reinforcer is given every time the youth displays the targeted behavior. A continuous schedule of reinforcement is critical when teaching a new behavior or skill to the student. You should reinforce the student each time the new behavior is performed to strengthen and encourage the use of the new behavior.

Once the behavior or skill has been established and consistent use is demonstrated, the reinforcement can move to an "intermittent schedule." On an intermittent schedule, targeted behaviors and skills are reinforced only some of the times they occur. For example, reinforcers may be provided every other time or every third time the behavior is performed, the first time the behavior occurs each hour, after two or three days of school attendance, or on any other schedule based on frequency or time. This may seem a bit contradictory, but intermittent schedules of reinforcement actually strengthen a behavior or skill more than continuous schedules. The element of surprise and not knowing when the reinforcer is coming keeps the student's performance of the behavior or skill occurring on a more consistent basis. Intermittent schedules of reinforcement also help fade (a concept that will be discussed later in the chapter) the consequences to a more reality-based schedule where reinforcers are not provided each time a youngster does something well.

Types of reinforcers

There are two basic types of reinforcers – primary and secondary. Primary reinforcers are unlearned events that, by virtue of their biological importance, serve as consequences that increase the likelihood the behavior that precedes them will occur again. Food, water, oxygen, and warmth are examples of events that do no have to undergo a process to make them reinforcing (Cooper, Heron, & Heward, 1987). In a state of deprivation, they reinforce behavior automatically. With primary reinforcers, it is not necessary for the individual to be aware that these events are reinforcing.

Secondary or "conditioned" reinforcers are neutral events that have acquired reinforcing potential because they have been matched (paired) with primary reinforcers or previously established secondary reinforcers. There are four kinds of secondary reinforcers:

1. Tangible reinforcers are objects or activities that increase the probability that the behavior preceding them will occur again. Some examples of tangible reinforcers are trinkets, pins, emblems, marbles, and toys.

2. Activity-oriented reinforcers are events or privileges such as helping the teacher, playing a game, or having lunch with an administrator. Many activity reinforcers do not have a direct cost so they can be used with programs that may not have the resources to purchase tangible reinforcers.

3. Social reinforcers maintain motivation to engage in appropriate behaviors on a daily basis. There are three kinds of social reinforcers. They are physical contacts (handshakes, pats on the back, etc.), proximity (standing or sitting near an individual), and verbal statements ("Good job," "Very good," etc.). Verbal statements can be either informational or affirmative. An example of an informational statement is, "Bobby, you carried your addition from the ones column to the tens column just as I had shown you. Good job!" Informational verbal statements describe specific behaviors. An example of an affirmative verbal statement is, "That was the correct answer." Affirmative verbal statements are more general in nature. However, both can be effective social reinforcers.

4. Generalized reinforcers are a type of conditioned reinforcer that does not rely on any sort of deprivation to be effective. Tokens, such as points in a motivation system, and money are two examples of generalized reinforcers. They allow the individual access to a wide array of other primary or secondary reinforcers. They also serve as an interim reinforcer to many others that are available at a later time. Those reinforcers that are available at a later time are called "back-up reinforcers." A benefit of using generalized reinforcers is that they can maintain behavior over extended time periods and are less likely to lead to satiation.

▶ Shaping

Behavioral shaping is defined as the differential reinforcement of successive approximations to a desired behavior (Alberto & Troutmann, 1990). In other words, shaping enhances the gradual development of a new behavior by continually reinforcing small improvements or steps toward the target behavior or goal. Rather than expecting a new behavior to occur exactly the way you taught it, you reinforce any behavior that closely resembles what you taught. Now let's

look specifically at differential reinforcement and successive approximations.

Differential reinforcement means that one behavior is reinforced while another behavior that was previously displayed is not. Both of these behaviors come from the same response class, which means they are similar or related behaviors.

Figure 2 illustrates a shaping process and how differential reinforcement is the key principle in use. The example is a shaping process that a teacher might use with a student who has a problem sitting up straight at his desk. This student frequently slouches down low in his seat. The step-by-step training progression starts with reinforcing the behavior of having the student's behind touching the desk chair. When that behavior is established, the student is reinforced for moving his behind closer to the back of the desk chair; he is not reinforced for only having his behind touching the chair. Next, the student is reinforced for having his lower back touching the back of the desk chair and the two previous behaviors are not reinforced. The shaping process continues until the student sits upright in the desk chair.

A successive approximation to a desired behavior is any intermediate behavior that is either part of the goal behavior or a combination of successive steps leading to the goal behavior. For example, successive approximations to the desired behavior of a student wearing his glasses all day at school might be first picking up the glasses, putting them on, wearing them for one class period, etc., until the student reaches his goal.

Some advantages of behavioral shaping:

1. It is a positive procedure because reinforcement is delivered consistently when the

Figure 2

Shaping Process

Differential reinforcement in action

Sitting upright in the desk

The lower back of the student is touching the back of the desk chair

Behind moves closer to the back of the desk chair

Behind is touching desk chair

The lower back of the student is touching the back of the desk chair

Behind moves closer to the back of the desk chair

Behind is touching desk chair

Behind moves closer to the back of the desk chair

Behind is touching desk chair

Behind is touching desk chair

Steps in differentially reinforcing sitting upright; shaded portion includes behaviors no longer reinforced.

successive approximations occur. The other behaviors that are displayed are not reinforced.

2. Shaping can be used to teach new behaviors. Because shaping is a gradual process, the end goal or desired behavior is always in sight. Shaping can be used with other behavior-building procedures.

Some disadvantages of behavioral shaping:

1. Shaping is a time-consuming process. Extended training with the student may be necessary before the final goal is met.

2. Progress in this process is not always an easy movement from one behavior to the next with uninterrupted flow. The student's behavior may become erratic, with considerable time lapses between movement. Certain steps may need to be further dissected into smaller steps so that smaller approximations can be mastered. This requires considerable monitoring to detect subtle indications that the next step in the sequence has been performed.

3. Because monitoring is time-consuming, it sometimes does not occur. This can make the whole shaping procedure ineffective and inefficient.

There are some guidelines that can be useful in making a behavioral shaping program effective and efficient:

1. Select the goal behavior. It is important to define the goal very specifically. The more behaviorally specific you can be, the greater the likelihood of success.

2. Decide the criteria for success. This should be specified so you can tell when the goal has been met. Some common criteria for success may include rate of behavior, frequency of behavior, percentage, magnitude, and duration.

3. Conduct a behavioral analysis of the goal behavior. Analyze each step in sequence that will have the end result of criterion performance of the goal.

4. Identify the first behavior to reinforce. The behavior should already occur at some minimal level. The behavior should be a member of the same response class of the goal behavior. By using these guidelines, you can begin reinforcing immediately and without waiting for a new behavior to occur spontaneously. The first behavior that is reinforced already has a direct link to the goal behavior, which moves the child closer to goal attainment.

5. Proceed in gradual steps. This is critical for success. The student's approximation of the goal dictates how quickly the goal is attained. Do not move ahead until a step is achieved or learned by the student.

6. Continue reinforcement when a desired behavior is achieved. If reinforcement is not continued, the behavior will be lost and the student's behavior will regress. Reinforce the behavior until the goal criterion is met and a schedule of reinforcement is established.

7. When at all possible, link the behavior to other behaviors. This will help the student be more productive at school and in other areas of his or her life.

▶ Fading

Fading refers to the gradual removal of antecedent prompts and cues so that naturally occurring events prompt the desired behavior. Fading is an important concept when artificial contingencies such as point systems are used with students in the classroom.

Here is an example of how fading is used in the classroom: One of your students loses a privilege each time she doesn't pay attention. As a prompt to pay attention, you start using a physical gesture such as looking directly at the student and then putting your finger to your eyes. The next step will be having the student pay attention without any prompting.

▶ Negative reinforcement

Negative reinforcement is another principle that is used to increase behavior. People often mistakenly think of negative reinforcement as a punishment procedure. This is not accurate because punishment procedures decrease behavior and negative reinforcement increases behavior. The term "negative" is used because the procedure removes or reduces, rather than creates or adds, an event. Negative reinforcement is the removal or the reduction of an ongoing event contingent upon a response, thus increasing the likelihood that the behavior will occur again under similar circumstances. The event that is removed is called the "negative reinforcer." Everyday examples of negative reinforcement include closing a window on a cold day or adjusting the flow of hot water in the shower. Because cold air coming through a window made you shiver in the past, or because water

that was too hot in the shower burned you, you remove these events to avoid the negative effect. Refer to Figure 1 for a review of this concept.

As an educator, your behavior is an important factor with regards to negative reinforcement. If you lose your teaching focus with students when they make a mistake, you may add to the potential of them not telling the truth about that situation. Yelling or making judgmental statements to a student who isn't following instructions and then asking about the situation may be unproductive. The student may lie in order to avoid or reduce the negative stimulus of the yelling or judgmental statements. In this situation, the student has nothing to lose by lying; if the student tells the truth, he or she will receive a consequence for what happened. On the other hand, if the student lies and you believe it, the student successfully avoids a consequence. The student is actually reinforced for lying.

There are two contingencies related to negative reinforcement. They are escape/escape and avoidance/avoidance (Cooper, Heron, & Heward, 1987).

Escape/escape stops an existing event. A teacher might be faced with a situation in which two students in class are loudly calling one another names, and this continues for a few minutes. The teacher might reprimand the students and tell them to stop the bickering. The students stop the bickering momentarily. The teacher now has been negatively reinforced for using reprimands because it stopped the bickering.

Avoidance/avoidance occurs when a person uses a behavior to avoid rather than terminate an event. A student might follow the teacher's instructions to avoid being sent to the office, or a student might sit in the back of the bus to avoid being teased by the other children on the bus. In each case, the student is escaping a negative stimulus.

▶ Positive punishment

To most people, the term punishment refers to the application of physical or psychological pain following the performance of a behavior. Generally, a person would think that a child who was spanked after running into the street had been punished for that behavior. However, the definition of punishment, as a principle of behavior, is the application of an aversive stimulus (following a behavior) that decreases the likelihood that a behavior will occur again. If the child does not run into the street again, then the spanking could be called punishment. However, if the spanking does not decrease the behavior, then it would not be considered punishment. Refer to Figure 1 for a review of the concept.

There are unconditioned and conditioned aversive stimuli. A stimulus that has not been previously experienced is an unconditioned aversive stimulus. For example: A loud blast or tone is sometimes used as an unconditioned stimulus to reduce the frequency of obscene phone calls. The caller has not been "conditioned," therefore, the unpleasantness of the stimulus may make the caller hang up.

A conditioned aversive stimulus is an event that is initially perceived as neutral, but by repeated pairing with an unconditioned aversive stimulus, becomes aversive in nature. An example is the word "No." It is not inherently aversive. However, continually pairing it with a loud, harsh voice can make "No" become aversive to students.

Three things must happen before something can be defined as punishment:

1. A behavior must be displayed.

2. The behavior must be followed by an aversive stimulus.

3. That stimulus alone must decrease the probability that the behavior will occur in the future.

The Boys Town Education Model does not rely on or recommend the use of "positive punishment" because it has many negative side effects. These include:

1. Negative reinforcement of the punisher. Not only is the person delivering the punishment negatively reinforced because the behavior ceases, but the student-educator relationship that is so necessary to internalizing behavior changes, is damaged. The educator will be more likely to use the same procedure in the future instead of trying something less restrictive.

2. Emotional or aggressive behavior. The student may attack, escape, or become physically aggressive toward the punisher in an effort to stop the punishment.

3. Avoidance and escape. Avoidance of the punisher can take a literal sense when students avoid the actual punishment or the place they were punished. For example, a student who is punished for being late to class may not go to class. Avoidance and escape behaviors also can occur in a nonliteral sense. For example, a student might escape punishing environments by taking drugs and alcohol, or by "tuning out" (Cooper, Heron, & Heward, 1987).

4. Negative modeling. If you punish a child for a behavior, the child will most likely imitate the punishment. Modeling punitive forms of behavior may negate the positive effects of your teaching.

5. Unpredictability. Side effects of punishment may be difficult to predict prior to implementing a treatment strategy. Persons utilizing the aversive stimuli should be aware of these effects and have an alternate plan for handling the situation.

Response cost/negative punishment

Response cost is a form of punishment in which a specific amount of reinforcement is lost as a result of an inappropriate behavior. As punishment, this decreases the probability that the behavior will occur again. A student losing part of his free time for not following your instructions or a student losing privileges because he did not complete his homework are examples of response cost. Refer to Figure 1 for a review of this concept.

There are three desirable aspects of using response cost. They are:

1. Similar to other forms of punishment, response cost usually produces a moderate-to-rapid decrease in behavior. Results of this procedure are apparent after a reasonable trial period, usually three to five days (Cooper, Heron, & Heward, 1987).

2. Response cost is a convenient procedure to use in the classroom. Many studies have shown that using these procedures results in a decrease in negative classroom behavior.

3. Response cost can be combined with other behavioral procedures in a comprehensive behavior-change program. In the Boys Town approach, the use of response cost is combined with the "fair pair" rule developed by White and Haring (1980). This rule suggests that the teacher reinforces one or more alternatives for every behavior targeted for reduction. It is critical to teach the prosocial alternative to any misbehavior and Boys Town's teaching techniques incorporate this concept. The combination of positive reinforcement and response cost helps to motivate the students to replace their misbehaviors with more appropriate behaviors.

The same conditions that impact the effectiveness of positive reinforcement also impact response cost: immediacy, choice of the reinforcer to be taken away, and withholding the reinforcer when a negative behavior occurs. Teachers are responsible for taking these conditions into account as they maximize the effectiveness of consequences they use for each individual student.

Extinction

Extinction is a procedure in which the reinforcement of a previously reinforced behavior is discontinued. Used in this way, extinction reduces behaviors that were previously maintained by positive and negative reinforcement and by naturally occurring sensory consequences.

Withholding reinforcers may easily be misused and may be seen as a student rights violation. Therefore, extinction should be used only after extensive consultation and only with administrative approval.

Generalization

Generalization means that skills learned in one set of antecedent conditions subsequently are used under different antecedent conditions. For example, skills learned in a classroom can be generalized to other appropriate environments outside the classroom. This principle of behavior means that each skill does not have to be taught in each new environment where it could be used. Generalization can be promoted by having the students thoroughly practice each skill and by conducting the practice under conditions that simulate the student's real environments (e.g., home, other classrooms, sports practices, recreation areas.). You can effectively promote generalization by monitoring how children are behaving in a variety of situations. This feedback, whether it be first- or second-hand observations, can give you opportunities to reinforce your students for generalizing appropriate behavior to new settings.

Discrimination

Discrimination means knowing that a behavior can be used in certain situations but not in others. For example, if a student uses slang with his friends, but uses proper grammar when talking with a teacher, he has appropriately discriminated between those situations. Similarly, aggression that is appropriate in an athletic contest is not appropriate in the classroom.

Much of the teaching done by educators not only helps students learn new skills but also teaches them where and under what conditions certain behaviors are appropriate. Teaching youth behavioral discrimina-

tion is crucial. They must learn to notice the environmental cues that call for different sets of behavior.

Summary

The principles of behavior discussed in this chapter form the foundation of the Boys Town Education Model.

Being an effective teacher is a challenging job. However, learning and applying these principles of behaviors will help reduce problems in your classrooms and help students solve some difficult behavior problems. By changing these maladaptive skills into prosocial behaviors, you are giving students a chance for success in their classrooms as well as success in their lives.

CHAPTER SIX

The social skills curriculum

"Teach your children well."

Deuteronomy 6:7

The Boys Town Education Model is made up of four components: the Social Skills Curriculum, Teaching Interactions, Motivation Systems, and Administrative Intervention. The Social Skills Curriculum tells us what to teach, while Teaching Interactions and Administrative Intervention provide the vehicle for teaching.

Combs and Slaby (1977) have defined a social skill as "the ability to interact with others... in ways that are socially accepted or valued and at the same time are personally beneficial or beneficial primarily to others." In the context of Catholic education, a social skill is something that helps a person get along with others in ways that match the values of the society and also meet the Church's expectations. The definition also suggests that social skills are not a constant set of behaviors, but vary according to the context in which they are to be used.

Using social skills in appropriate ways, across a variety of situations, is a very complex process. It involves more that knowing a set of behaviors; rather, it is a rapid chain of decisions based on reading cues and determining responses in the context of inter-personal interactions.

At first glance, one might wonder what in the world greeting skills have to do with moral or spiritual development. Think for a moment, though. Isn't the importance of spiritual values wrapped up in the quality of relationships we each have with others? (Remember the Golden Rule.) If so, then what more logical way to begin than by teaching young people the skills necessary to build healthy, high-quality relationships. These skills can empower youth to begin to act and to live in a new way.

In fact, the beauty of a skills-based approach to moral/spiritual development for young people is evident in the fact that as the youth put these skills into practice, relationships become more meaningful. In short, the human need for relationships drives a skills-based spirituality that is rooted in caring – caring for self, caring for others, allowing others to care for you, and caring about your relationship with God (Higher Power). The Ten Commandments are an example of the need to care for ourselves, others, and our relationship with God.

The first three Commandments concern our relationship with God.

1. "I am the Lord, your God, you shall not have other gods besides me."

2. "You shall not take the name of the Lord, your God, in vain."

3. "Remember to keep Holy the Sabbath."

The next seven Commandments concern our relationship with others.

4. "Honor your Father and Mother, that you may have a long life in the world which the Lord, your God, is giving you."

5. "Thou shalt not kill."

6. "Thou shalt not commit adultery."

7. "Thou shalt not steal."

8. "Thou shalt not bear false witness against thy neighbor."

9. "Thou shalt not covet thy neighbor's wife."

10. "Thou shalt not covet thy neighbor's goods."

This brings us to the first principle in moral formation: the degree to which human beings, including young people, develop a personal relationship to Jesus Christ as Savior and Lord and the degree to which a strong foundation is being built for their appropriate moral and spiritual growth and development. It is imperative that this growth and development be rooted in the Ten Commandments and the Beatitudes, which Jesus gave us in the Sermon on the Mount.

While the Ten Commandments are the basic framework, or foundation, recognized by all three great religions in the word – Judaism, Islam, and Christianity – the Beatitudes give us direction in how to implement these "laws of faith" in our lives. In other words, the Beatitudes answer the question, "What more must I do to be a follower of Jesus?" The Beatitudes do nothing more and nothing less than specify what results when you combine a personal relationship with Jesus as Savior and Lord with a moral foundation based on the Ten Commandments.

Literally dozens of skills would need to be taught to a young person in order to equip him or her with the ability to live out all of these Commandments. These skills are just the starting place for young people who are seeking to make some practical sense of a spiritual life that affects everyday relationships. In learning and practicing these skills, young people are empowering themselves to live out faith in ways that they may not have thought possible.

Teachers in Catholic schools and Catholic school systems have the unique opportunity to reach students by combining religious, human, and academic development. This moral blending can be greatly enhanced by a strong social skills curriculum.

Catholic educators stand firm in the belief that our schools are to be mediators both of culture and faith. One does not exclude the other. In fact, each discipline is meant to be central to our Catholic mission.

A social skills curriculum is a framework for teaching our children how to behave in a multitude of situations. When children are given options for appropriate behavior, they feel more secure and can get along better with peers and adults. Actually, actively teaching social skills to our students gives them "survival skills" for life's rough spots.

Children who lack social skills are more likely to experience difficulties in school and beyond. Children who have difficulty with certain kinds of social behavior, especially paying attention, persevering, volunteering, and communicating with teachers, may be at risk for academic failure (Stephens, 1978) and peer acceptance problems (Schneider & Byrne, 1984). The link between poor social skills and other problems is clear. Gresham (1981) found that children with social skill deficits experienced a variety of problems, including aggressive and antisocial behavior, juvenile delinquency, learning problems and school failure, mental health disorders, and loneliness and despondency.

The teaching of social skills, then, becomes imperative if we truly are committed to helping students achieve success in school and beyond. Teachers in Catholic schools are a powerful influence on children, serving as role models of acceptable social behavior and moral and spiritual values. Escalating moral problems such as greed, violence, drugs, and suicide fuel the need for a religion-based curriculum. Historically, teachers have not engaged in purposeful teaching of social skills; instead, it often has existed as a "hidden curriculum." Teachers set standards and held students accountable for meeting them. Without a certain number of rules and expectations, classrooms couldn't run successfully. Without behavioral guidelines, group teaching would be impossible.

When a student is in the early stages of learning skills, a considerable amount of compliance is required in order for him or her to understand and benefit from your teaching. The student needs the "building blocks" of the basic skills to develop the higher-level skills that lead to self-reliance and self-efficacy. Once students begin to experience success using the basic skills you have taught, their beliefs about their capabilities to use those skills start to change. These beliefs or judgments about our abilities to influence the events that impact our lives are critical to our successes – more so than our actual skill levels (Mager, 1992). By giving students the basic tools of social interaction, we can shape success experiences and help them utilize learned skills to broaden and deepen their social skill repertoire.

"These young people absorb a wide and varied assortment of knowledge from all kinds of sources, including the school. But they are not yet capable of ordering or prioritizing what they have learned. Often enough, they do not yet have the critical ability needed to distinguish the true and the good from their opposites; they have not yet acquired the necessary religious and moral criteria that will enable them to remain objective and independent when faced with the prevailing attitudes and habits of society. Concepts such as truth, beauty, and goodness have become so vague today that young people do not know where to turn to find help; even when they are able to hold on to certain values, they do not yet have the capacity to develop these values into a way of life; all too often they are more inclined simply to go their own way, accepting whatever is popular at the moment." (The Religious Dimension of Education in a Catholic School, 9)

Some private and public schools have also been known for their enforcement of strict rules and guidelines. Unfortunately, many of these rules, guidelines, and expectations serve to control the behavior of students instead of empowering them to make responsible decisions. Although we need a certain number of compliance-based rules to ensure smooth classroom operation, we can achieve the greatest good by helping students learn to make responsible choices about their own behavior and act in accordance with Catholic doctrine. Doing so provides them with tools for meeting future challenges, in addition to helping them succeed in school today.

Our boys and girls need to know that their happiness and success is to know, love, and serve God, with all their hearts, minds, and souls and to love their neighbors as themselves. Teachers need to unabashedly teach this truth. Knowing this truth will help children to acquire virtues, to think critically, and to develop morally, academically, and socially. Teachers who work in a Catholic school must be persons of faith who can guide young people in the tenets of our church, the sacred Scriptures, and the sacraments. And through teaching life skills and building relationships, teachers can help students develop their ability to choose right over wrong, good over bad.

▶ Curriculum skills in the Catholic school

The reason for teaching social skills that we give to our students should reflect social responsibilities and concern for others, and religious faith as well as personal benefits or negative consequences. Our culture vigorously promotes a self-centered, immediate gratification theme. Boys Town's Social Skill Curriculum is the bridge between social and spiritual values that are rooted in God and love of neighbor. Students need to know that following instructions and raising their hands before speaking shows concern for others' time and respect for authority. Giving students these kinds of rationales promotes the social-spiritual continuum.

Giving students reasons for engaging in social skills may not convince them to use social skills, but it will show them practical ways to succeed at school, at home, and at work. It also improves their relationship with their peers as you teach them to move from self-centered motives to other- and God-centered virtues. The Social Skills Curriculum gives kids "cues" in social situations and options for making decisions.

It is difficult to teach Catholic virtues to today's children. We compete with a culture that is full of sex, drugs, suicide, fast cash, obscenity-laced music, and violent movies. We can't take kids out of the world or our culture, but we can make sure they are exposed to the Christian perspective along with a practical curriculum of social skills.

Deuteronomy 6:6-7 reminds us: "These commandments that I give you today are to be upon your hearts. Impress them on your children. Talk about them when you sit and when you walk along the road, when you lie down, and when you get up."

Talk about these commandments of justice and of love regardless of what subject you teach or where you happen to be when you're talking to your students. Tell your students of God's love for them as they enter or exit your classroom.

Children's attention spans have been shaped by video games, virtual reality, and TV commercials with three-second sound bites. Students' responses to a social skill curriculum founded on a faith-base may be apathy, sarcasm, or defensiveness. While the competition is formidable, our inheritance is strong and Christ still speaks to young hearts through your work as teachers. As servant teachers, you must be creative, energetic, and nonapologetic. It will challenge every fiber of your heart, but in the end, you will see dramatic changes, as hundreds of your fellow colleagues have seen.

Sixteen skills make up the curriculum. They encompass four main areas: adult relations, peer relations, school rules, and classroom behaviors. The 16 skills are divided into two categories, **Basic** and **Advanced**.

The seven basic skills have been designated as "basic" because of their level of simplicity and because they come into play so frequently during the course of any given day. Since a large percentage of our daily social interactions are covered by these basic skills, they often are referred to as critical skills. Mastering these seven skills, along with learning effective conversation skills can significantly improve a student's ability to succeed in school. If students can adequately perform in these areas, they'll not only avoid

considerable conflict with adults and peers, but also will have some prosocial skills that will enable them to make and keep friends, and maintain better relationships.

Basic skills

1. Following instructions
2. Accepting criticism or a consequence
3. Accepting "No" for an answer
4. Greeting others
5. Getting the teacher's attention
6. Making a request
7. Disagreeing appropriately

Advanced skills

8. Giving criticism
9. Resisting peer pressure
10. Making an apology
11. Talking with others
12. Giving compliments
13. Accepting compliments
14. Volunteering
15. Reporting other youths' behavior
16. Introducing yourself

The following section lists the 16 skills and their steps. These skills also are included in the Appendix at the end of this manual.

► Social skills for students

Basic skills

Skill 1

Following instructions

1. Look at the person.
2. Say "Okay."
3. Do what you've been asked right away.
4. Check back.

Skill 2

Accepting criticism or a consequence

1. Look at the person.
2. Say "Okay."
3. Don't argue.

Skill 3

Accepting "No" for an answer

1. Look at the person.
2. Say "Okay."
3. Stay calm.
4. If you disagree, ask later.

Skill 4

Greeting others

1. Look at the person.
2. Use a pleasant voice.
3. Say "Hi" or "Hello."

Skill 5

Getting the teacher's attention

1. Look at the teacher.
2. Raise your hand. Stay calm.
3. Wait until the teacher says your name.
4. Ask your question.

Skill 6

Making a request

1. Look at the person.
2. Use a clear, pleasant voice.
3. Explain exactly what you are asking for. Say "Please."
4. If the answer is "Yes," say "Thank you."
5. If not, remember to accept "No" for an answer.

Skill 7

Disagreeing appropriately

1. Look at the person.
2. Use a pleasant voice.
3. Say "I understand how you feel."
4. Tell why you feel differently.
5. Give a reason.
6. Listen to the other person.

Advanced skills

Skill 8
Giving criticism

1. Look at the person.
2. Stay calm. Use a pleasant voice.
3. Say something positive, or "I understand."
4. Describe exactly what you are criticizing.
5. Tell why this is a problem.
6. Listen to the person. Be polite.

Skill 9
Resisting peer pressure

1. Look at the person.
2. Use a calm voice.
3. Say clearly that you do not want to participate.
4. Suggest something else to do.
5. If necessary, continue to say "No."
6. Leave the situation.

Skill 10
Making an apology

1. Look at the person.
2. Use a serious, sincere voice.
3. Say "I'm sorry for... " or "I want to apologize for...."
4. Don't make excuses.
5. Explain how you plan to do better in the future.
6. Say "Thanks for listening."

Skill 11
Talking with others

1. Look at the person.
2. Use a pleasant voice.
3. Ask questions.
4. Don't interrupt.

Skill 12
Giving compliments

1. Look at the person.
2. Smile.
3. Speak clearly and enthusiastically.
4. Tell the person exactly what you like.

Skill 13
Accepting compliments

1. Look at the person.
2. Use a pleasant voice.
3. Say "Thank you."
4. Don't look away, mumble, or refuse a compliment.
5. Do not disagree with the compliment.

Skill 14
Volunteering

1. Look at the person.
2. Use a pleasant, enthusiastic voice.
3. Ask if you can help. Describe the activity or task you are offering to do.
4. Thank the person.
5. Check back when you have finished.

Skill 15

Reporting other youths' behavior

1. Look at the teacher or adult.
2. Use a calm voice. Ask to talk to him or her privately.
3. Describe the inappropriate behavior you are reporting.
4. Explain why you are making the report.
5. Answer any questions the adult has.
6. Thank the adult for listening.

Skill 16

Introducing yourself

1. Look at the person. Smile.
2. Use a pleasant voice.
3. Offer a greeting. Say "Hi, my name is...."
4. Shake the person's hand.
5. When you leave, say, "It was nice to meet you."

Remember that not all of the expected behaviors may be clearly spelled out in the steps of each skill. Some specific teaching regarding the quality of a student's voice, the manner in which he or she uses eye contact, and other "paraskill" behaviors may be necessary to enhance a student's success. In other words, when teaching a social skill to a student, you need to teach the individual steps that make up the skill and the various behaviors that make up each step. For example:

Following instructions

Step
Look at the person.

Behavior
Look directly at the person without glaring or making faces.

Step
Say "Okay."

Behavior
Answer right away. Speak clearly without sounding angry.

Step
Do the task immediately.

Behavior
Start doing the task within two or three seconds. Keep at the task until it's done. Ask for help if there are problems.

Step
Check back.

Behavior
Report what was done as soon as the task is completed. Correct anything that needs to be done again.

An excellent source for defining exact expectations for a variety of social skills is *Teaching Social Skills to Youth : A Curriculum for Child-Care Providers* (Dowd & Tierney, 1992). Many of the behavioral examples presented in this chapter were drawn from that text.

Although the Social Skills Curriculum consists of only 16 skills, you can teach any skill by task-analyzing it and teaching it in a step-by-step manner. Start by deciding what you want the student to do. That is, begin with the end in mind. Once you know your end product, determine exactly what behaviors need to be included to get the desired result. Make sure each step is observable so you can tell whether the student is meeting your expectations. Include only critical steps, as you don't want the skill to be so long that neither you nor the student can remember all the components. For example, you may come up with the following steps for a skill you call "How to Stay On Task":

1. Begin working as soon as the assignment is given.

2. Continue working until the assignment is completed or time runs out.

3. Get the teacher's attention appropriately if you need help or when your assignment is done.

Remember that the level of skill performance will vary among students, depending upon their skill levels and the areas that you target for teaching. You might expect a higher skilled student to respond to criticism by following the skill steps exactly, but your tolerances for a student who is just beginning the program would most likely be quite a bit different. For example, you may accept a new student's response of rolling his eyes and looking away while hearing your criticism because when he first joined your classroom, he argued loudly and turned away from you. His new behaviors indicate considerable improvement and progress. Even though the behavior does not match your "ultimate" expectations, you can continue to

shape the student's behavior by individualizing your teaching.

▶ Introducing the Social Skills Curriculum

A social skills program can be taught like any other curriculum. Each skill should be taught individually at a neutral time (see Chapter 10 "Preventive Teaching") to help students experience success and gain fluency with the skills. At the same time, your students will be engaged in "on-the-job" training since you will be addressing behaviors as they occur.

Prioritize your skill instruction by assessing the needs of your students. Skills that must be used frequently or are in need of improvement will probably be among the first ones you will focus on. Keep in mind that the value of any social skill may vary according to who is assessing its importance. Your level of interest in fostering development of certain social skills may be much higher than that of your students. Whereas you may view a particular skill as central to effective classroom operation (for example, "How to Accept a 'No' Answer"), your students may have a different point of view. They may feel their status among their peers is endangered by performing the skill steps you have outlined. So, the manner in which you select and teach social skills should take the child's perspective into consideration, along with your own, for greatest impact and effectiveness (Dowd & Tierney, 1992).

Following your needs assessment, you will teach the social skills much like you would any other content area. To be effective, you will teach and practice the skills, then assess, redirect, and reinforce student efforts. By setting aside a regular block of time to preteach and practice skills, you will communicate to students that learning social skills is as important as any other subject in school.

Equally critical to the success of the program is your consistent follow-up with each student. Immediate and contingent reinforcement and Corrective Teaching® emphasize the importance of the Social Skills Curriculum and take advantage of the "teachable moment." Addressing behavior as it occurs enhances the learning environment by making the learning relevant and immediate.

Ideally, praise should occur four times as often as Corrective Teaching for change to take place most quickly. Noticing positive behaviors not only sends the message that you are aware of the "good" things your students do, but also helps you build and maintain relationships with each student.

When teaching social skills, your behavior is extremely important. Whether praising appropriate behavior or effort, or teaching alternatives to inappropriate behavior, your demeanor and disposition should be supportive and calm. Looking at the student, using the student's name, maintaining a pleasant and neutral voice tone and facial expression, placing yourself on the student's physical plane (i.e., both sitting or both standing), and keeping a comfortable distance between you and the student all contribute to the quality of the interaction. Your behavior sets the tone of the interaction and greatly affects the outcome of your attempts to teach social skills. (See Chapter 9, "Effective Praise," for additional discussion.)

Finally, use the teaching techniques described in Chapters 9 through 12 to effectively motivate behavioral change. The sequences are designed to facilitate social skills learning by maintaining a teaching focus. Without each of the specific components, your interactions could become vague, irrelevant, or punitive. If you remember that the emphasis is on teaching, you are more likely to have a positive impact on your students' behavior. Clear, consistent social skills teaching can only increase the likelihood that your students will learn new behaviors.

▶ Modeling social skills

Being a living example, St. Paul urged young Timothy to "set an example for the believers in speech, in life, in love, in faith, and in purity" (1 Timothy 4:12). This doesn't mean we never make any mistakes. It means that if God is in our hearts and in our lives, we will live in a way that our students can be drawn to. A teacher's example can help shape the character of our children.

As God has been to you, so you must be to your students. As He has dealt with you, so you must deal with them. Such kindness as He has shown you, such patience, such intolerance of sin – these must you in turn show to those for whom you stand in place of God. Each time your students see a God-like attitude, skill, or action, the Holy Spirit will tell them, "Now you can understand a little better what your Father in Heaven is like."

▶ Summary

The 16 skills in the Boys Town Education Model form the basic curriculum for teaching social behavior. Skills are made up of a number of observable steps and are categorized as Basic and Advanced. Any behavior can be broken down into components and taught in a systematic manner to meet each student's needs. Skills should be taught preventively so that students know what your expectations are, and also in response to negative behaviors as they occur. Teaching sequences and strategies will be presented in later chapters.

CHAPTER SEVEN

Observing and describing behavior

The foundation of effective teaching is the ability to observe and describe behavior. This skill helps you determine what effect you have on your students and how their behavior affects you. It also helps you identify what skills to teach students and what behaviors make up each skill.

The goal of observing and describing behavior is to accurately verbalize what is happening in a given situation. In fact, the best descriptions are those that mirror a person's behavior so clearly that the behavior could be repeated or reenacted by someone who hadn't observed the behavior firsthand.

Changing the inappropriate behaviors of students and teaching new, appropriate behaviors is made easier by the ability to observe and describe behavior.

▶ Observing behavior

The first step in observing and describing any behavior is to watch and listen carefully. Determine who was involved in the situation and attend specifically to the following areas:

What the person is doing. Look at both large and small body movements, such as running, walking, kicking, throwing, hand gestures, and body posture.

Facial expressions help you determine a student's feelings. Look for expressions – smiles, scowls, grimaces, stares, or rolling of the eyes or eye contact.

What the person is saying. Listen carefully to specific words and how they are said. Voice tone and inflection can sometimes be better indicators of what a youth is feeling than the words that are used. Also notice giggles, groans, moans, or sighs.

Frequency, intensity, and duration of the behavior. These characteristics often determine whether a behavior is appropriate or inappropriate. Monitor whether the behavior occurs too frequently or not frequently enough, whether it escalates in intensity, and whether it lasts too long or not long enough.

When and where the behavior occurs. What events and circumstances happen before the behavior happens? What time of day does it occur and where does it take place? For example, laughing with a friend in the hallway may be appropriate; laughing with a friend during study hall may be inappropriate.

The absence of behavior. Was there a behavior that should have occurred but did not? For example, did the student fail to look at another person during conversation, or not answer a question when asked, or fail to raise his hand before speaking in class?

▶ Describing behavior

After closely observing behaviors, begin forming a mental picture of what occurred – almost like an instant replay of the behavior. Your goal is to describe what happened as accurately as possible. Concentrate solely on what behaviors occurred. An accurate picture of the situation is needed before any successful intervention is attempted. Don't make any judgments based on a student's intentions or motives.

Make your descriptions:

1. Specific

2. Behavioral

3. Objective

Specific – Avoid using adjectives that are general or vague. You may feel that a student has a "bad attitude," but what behaviors did the student engage in that gave you this impression? Similarly, a "good job," may indicate general satisfaction, but what specifically was good about it? The goal of being specific is to give students messages that are easily understood and that convey exactly what you mean. A "good job" may be more accurately described as using complete sentences on an essay test, completing a difficult classroom assignment on time, or putting all supplies where they belong without being prompted. The more specific you can be, the more likely it is that the student will understand; this creates an opportunity for the student to repeat positive behavior or change negative behavior.

One way to describe behavior accurately is to concentrate on using action verbs instead of adjectives. For example, terms like "You ran," "You growled," or "You yelled" describe actions and are easy to understand. They are not as vague as descriptions that rely solely on adjectives, e.g., good, bad, unfriendly, antisocial, etc.

Behavioral – Break behaviors down into specific components. For example, being "antisocial" could be described as not speaking when spoken to, avoiding participation in study groups with other students, showing disinterest in extracurricular events, and so on. In this way, the student has three specific areas where he or she could learn new social skills.

Objective – Judgmental terms can harm a relationship by damaging a student's self-esteem or triggering an emotional reaction. Terms like "stupid," "bad," and "terrible" should be avoided. Also, keep any negative emotions under control. Concentrate on using a calm, matter-of-fact approach when describing behavior. Stay objective and students will be more likely to view you as concerned, pleasant, and fair. For example, instead of saying, "You were disrespectful to me," you could say, "When I asked you for your book, you scowled and gestured with your finger."

When describing verbal behavior, you may sometimes need to repeat exactly what a student says (within ethical and moral limits, of course). If you cannot offer an exact quote, begin your description with "You said something like...." Carefully and specifically describing verbal behavior helps you remain objective and concentrate on observable events and behaviors.

▶ When to observe and describe behavior

Naturally, observing and describing behavior is an ongoing process whenever you are working with your students. However, there are times when you will want to "zero in" on certain behaviors. These times include:

When the student's behavior is inappropriate. This could include any form of misbehavior or problem behavior, such as not following an instruction, arguing, or complaining.

When the student's behavior is particularly appropriate. This is a special time to "catch 'em being good" – to focus on behavior that you want to occur again. Many of us usually are so locked in to dealing only with problem behaviors that we often neglect to find something to praise and then tell the student about it. Describing what your students are doing correctly helps develop relationships and reinforce positive behavior.

When you want to teach a new skill. Describing new behaviors helps students learn quicker and progress through academic and social curricula more efficiently. Accurately describing what was done, both correctly and incorrectly, gives the student feedback on his or her performance that is valuable in internalizing the skill you are teaching.

The ability to observe and describe behavior is a valuable skill. Accurate, objective descriptions help establish expectations and ensure successful and comfortable learning experiences for the student.

▶ Integrating behavioral descriptions and skill labels

The Teaching Interaction – a nine-step method used at Boys Town to teach skills to students – will be explained in detail in

Chapter 11. For now, it is important to present an explanation of how observing and describing behaviors fits into this teaching method. Clearly describing behavior and labeling skills help you teach your students a great deal in a short time. Clear, behavioral descriptions and skill labels are integrated into most of the components of Teaching Interactions.

An example of using skill labels and behavioral descriptions in the first three steps of a Teaching Interaction follows. Learning how to specifically describe behavior and label skills while using these steps will provide clear, focused, and non-judgmental teaching to your students. Explanations for each step also are provided.

Example

Situation: Chris, a new student, is working on the computer during study hour. His teacher asks Chris to open the window to let some fresh air into the classroom. Chris sighs, doesn't look at the teacher, but gets up and walks to the window. The use of the first four steps might sound something like this:

Initial praise or empathy

Teacher: *"Chris, you did a good job of getting right up to open the window. I know it's hard to follow instructions sometimes, especially when you're working on the computer."*

Explanation: Specific, descriptive praise is given for "getting right up...." The general skill is identified in the context of the empathy statement, "I know it's hard to follow instructions...." Whenever possible, the initial praise should relate to behaviors that are part of the skill being praised or taught.

Description of the inappropriate behavior

Teacher: *"But just now when I gave you that instruction, you sighed and you didn't look at me or say anything to let me know you heard or that you would help out."*

Explanation: Note that the general skill category of "Following Instructions" is repeated and the observed inappropriate behavior is described. Also, note that the teacher avoids vague and judgmental descriptions such as, "You weren't very cooperative..." or "You didn't seem too happy when I asked you to...."

Description of the appropriate behavior

Teacher: *"Chris, let's talk about following instructions. Whenever anyone gives you an instruction, whether it's a teacher, your parents, or your employer, there are several things you should do.*

You need to look at the person and answer him or her by saying 'Okay' or 'Sure' to let the person know you're listening and will follow through. Be sure to ask questions if you don't understand. Do the task and then check back with the person when it's completed."

Explanation: The teacher helps the youth generalize the skill to other situations by explaining the antecedent condition, "Whenever anyone gives you an instruction...." Then, the teacher provides a step-by-step, behavioral description to help the student learn the skill. During an actual interaction, the teacher would pause frequently to ask the student if he or she understands, has any questions, etc.

▶ Summary

Educators can be pleasant and effective by following the guidelines for describing behavior (carefully observing antecedents, behavior, and consequences); labeling skills and describing the behaviors related to them; and skillfully integrating these techniques into the components of all teaching techniques: Preventive Teaching, Effective Praise, and the Teaching Interaction.

Rationales

Most of us are familiar with the phrase, "Do it because I said so"; it's the "reason" adults often gave us when we were growing up. As adults, we have said the same thing to our own kids or our students. However, research tells us that children learn more, and are more willing to learn, when given reasons that explain how a behavior will affect them. The Boys Town Education Model employs this reality; it directs educators to use rationales when teaching their students.

A rationale, by definition, is a fundamental reason. We use rationales in many ways everyday to explain the benefits or drawbacks of maintaining or changing a behavior. For example, a simple rationale for practicing a sport is that your team will probably do better in a game. A rationale for being on time for work is that your employer appreciates punctuality and may take that into consideration when deciding whether to give you a raise. A rationale for dieting is that you will lose weight.

In the Boys Town Education Model, educators use rationales to show students how a behavior is linked to what happens as a result of the behavior. In a Teaching Interaction, a rationale is provided to describe the effect a behavior could have on others. It may also describe the possible benefits or negative consequences a student might receive for engaging in a certain behavior. For example, you might tell a youngster that he should follow instructions to complete an assignment so he will have more free time to do a fun activity. You might tell a student that the reason she should study hard is to improve her grades. Or, you might tell a student who is calling other children names that no one will want to play with him if the name-calling continues.

Many students, older as well as younger, don't understand the relationship between what they do and the consequences that follow. Giving rationales to students plays a critical part in teaching social, academic, and religious principles. "Why?" is a good question for students to ask. "Because I said so," is a poor and irresponsible answer for teachers to give in response.

When teachers give students rationales that cover the full social and spiritual spectrum, it provides a foundation for moral and social awareness and development. Using rationales to explain to students how behavior is connected to the end result is pivotal to any teaching approach. Teachers need to rethink their lesson plans if they can't give sound reasons for what they are teaching.

In Catholic schools, many rationales focus on sensitivity and concern for others, not self. Children need to understand that their behavior leaves an impression on other people and those impressions reflect on their parents, their teachers, and everyone in the school. The messages in today's society tell kids to "live it up," or if "it feels good, do it." Kids also are bombarded with messages that imply that it's okay to worship material things. Even bumper stickers sell a materialistic view: "He who dies with the most toys wins." The signs of our times bode disaster if kids don't hear intrinsic guidelines and religious principles as reasons for moral behavior.

Many students have been cut off from the very power in their lives that can help them discover meaning and purpose in life. It is the role of all educators in Catholic schools to teach social skills and faith skills in order to form a foundation upon which stu-

dents can construct a moral life. Rationales play an integral role in helping students learn practical and moral reasons for using these skills.

▶ Types of rationales

Rationales fall into four main categories: benefits, negative consequences, concern-for-others, and faith-based. Ultimately, your goal for all students is to teach them to consider the implications of their behavior on others. As such, it is important to incorporate rationales that focus on concern for others. It is also important to deliver as many faith-oriented rationales as possible in order to reinforce the moral and spiritual lessons taught by the Catholic Church. Some students may not respond immediately to these types of reasons, either because they don't understand them or because they haven't experienced situations that are meaningful to them. In those cases, students may be more likely to respond to rationales that explain what the students will gain by using certain behaviors.

A **benefits** rationale answers the questions of "What's in it for me?" or "How can it help me?" These may reflect the benefits or positive outcomes that might logically occur when a student engages in appropriate behavior or avoids engaging in inappropriate behavior. For example, a benefit statement may be, "When you can get a teacher's attention appropriately, you'll be more likely to get the help you need quickly and can then finish your work faster." A rationale for avoiding inappropriate behavior might sound like, "When you don't tease others, they're more likely to want to be around you and include you in games or activities." Both types of rationales point out a potential gain or benefit to the student. Benefits rationales, as mentioned earlier, tend to be the most powerful or meaningful to children. This is especially true for students who are less developmentally mature or who are new to a social skills program.

A **negative consequences** rationale, on the other hand, states the potential negative outcomes associated with engaging in inappropriate behavior. "How can I be hurt?" or "What price might I have to pay?" are questions that are answered by a negative consequences rationale. Examples include: "When you don't turn assignments in, you get further behind, your grade drops, and you could even fail the class," or "If you argue when you're corrected, you may not get the help you need and may repeat the same mistakes," or "If you don't smile and return someone's greeting, the person may think you're unfriendly or rude, and may begin to avoid you instead of trying to be your friend." Although negative consequences are sometimes the most logical ones to point out, frequent use may be interpreted as verbal warnings or threats. This type of rationale, therefore, should be used selectively.

A **concern-for-others** rationale states the effects a youth's behavior may have on other people. In addition to teaching students to care for and respect those who could be affected by the students' actions, this type of rationale incorporates the notion of consideration for the rights and property of others. Examples include: "If you call out to get a teacher's attention, you could disturb others who are trying to complete their assignments," and "When you tease other students,

they may take you seriously and their feelings may be hurt." As mentioned earlier, concern-for-others rationales may not be effective with some of your students at first. Some students, because of age, developmental level, or personal needs, are unable to consider the rights, feelings, or needs of others. Therefore, a gradual introduction of this type of rationale into the teaching process, especially as the child is demonstrating behavioral gains, may be a more effective approach.

"A Catholic school should be sensitive to and help to promulgate Church appeals for peace, justice, freedom, progress for all peoples and assistance for countries in need." (The Religious Dimension of Education in a Catholic School, 45) Treating people fairly and justly is the least one can do for others; loving another person is the most one can do. By teaching other-centered rationales, you teach students to begin to respect and treat others fairly.

Faith-based rationales teach young people how to build healthy relationships that are rooted in their relationship with God and respect for self and for others. At the very core of this basic principle is the Golden Rule itself – "Do unto others what you would have them do unto you" – a form of which can be found in the sacred writings of all of the world's major religions.

▶ The Golden Rule according to the world's major religions

Buddhism

"Do not offend others as you would not wish to be offended."

Undanavarga

Confucianism

"Is there a maxim that one ought to follow all his life?

Surely the maxim of peaceful goodness: What we don't want done to us we should not do to others."

Analects

Judaism

"What you don't wish for yourself, do not wish for your neighbor. This is the law, the rest is only commentary."

Talmud Shabbat

Christianity

"Do unto others as you would have them do unto you."

St. Matthew

Islam

"Not one of you will be a true believer who does not wish for his brother the same that he wishes for himself."

Sunnatt

Taoism

"Hold as your own the gains of your neighbor and as yours his losses."

T'ai-Shang Kan-Ying P'ien

Many of the rationales that you provide for students will center around these basic rules for getting along with others. These people could be their classmates or peers, teachers, coaches, parents, ministers, and so on.

▶ Rationales and consequences

Combining rationales and consequences is an effective way to teach skills. Providing children with rationales that point out how their behavior affects other people helps enhance a student's moral awareness and development. According to Damon (1988), the "optimal conditions for the successful induction of moral beliefs are (1) control of the child's behavior through the minimal external force necessary for achieving such control, combined with (2) provision of information to the child about the rationale for the standard through persuasion, argument, and reasoning." The goal is to have the student engage in the appropriate behavior and then to come away from the event remembering why it is important to do so. This is only possible if the informational message (or rationale) is more memorable to the child than the consequences for the behavior.

The key is presenting a moral rationale (or other-centered rationale) along with the least-restrictive consequence so that the child mainly retains the rationale. An example might be a situation where a student inappropriately yells out for the teacher's help on an assignment. Combining an other-centered rationale such as, "Getting the teacher's attention by quietly raising your hand won't disturb the other students around you," along with a severe consequence like a detention after school will cause the student to remember only the consequence and not the rationale of the importance of engaging in the appropriate behavior. Using a less-restrictive consequence such as loss of computer or recess time will help the child focus on the rationale instead of the consequence. Keep in mind that there are many factors to consider –

the age of the youth, developmental level, skill deficiencies, frequency and severity of the problem behavior – when determining the appropriateness of a consequence. Using the least-restrictive consequence along with pertinent rationales produces the optimal conditions for children to learn and internalize various moral standards.

▶ Benefits of using rationales

As mentioned earlier, rationales that stress a concern for others can enhance moral awareness and development. According to Damon (1988), "moral education efforts in and out of school have a cumulative effect not so much because the child benefits from hearing the same thing more than once but because morality is largely a matter of adapting fundamental values to a variety of social contexts. As children experience moral thoughts and feelings in diverse social settings, their moral awareness expands correspondingly. Moreover, children's natural moral reactions are strengthened through the pluralistic social support that becomes available through many different types of peer and adult-child relations." When schools stress and teach students appropriate skills with rationales that emphasize a concern for others, it enhances the moral education being provided at home and helps increase and strengthen a child's moral awareness and development.

Using rationales also helps adults build positive relationships with children. Pikas (1961) and Willner, Braukmann, Kirigin, Fixsen, Phillips, and Wolf (1977) found that youth prefer adults who give rationales and explanations with their disciplinary requests.

For example, youth would prefer the statement, "You can't watch television right now because your homework is not finished," which contains a rationale, over the statement, "You can't watch television right now."

Rationales also can help with compliance. Elder (1963) found that youngsters are more likely to comply with their parent's requests if the parents provide explanations for their rules and requests. For example, a parent might say, "If you save your money from your paper route, then together we can buy a new bike." This statement contains a rationale implying that the youngster cannot have a new bicycle now and why he or she should save money. Elder also found that when parents provided rationales for rules and requests, their children were more likely to be confident in their own ideas and opinions. This confidence, along with the youngsters' understanding of the relationship between their behavior and the consequences, can help youth make better decisions.

Because rationales help youth understand the relationship between their behavior and the subsequent consequences, your students can gain insight about the importance of learning new skills to replace old behaviors. As a result, children become less dependent on external rewards and reinforcement to motivate behavior change because they see how their behavior determines what happens to them.

With regard to Teaching Interactions, Willner et al. (1977) and Braukmann, Ramp, Braukmann, Willner, and Wolf (1983) found that youngsters prefer Teaching Interactions in which adults provide explanations as they teach alternative, more appropriate skills. They found that when adults use rationales, youth are more likely to view them as fair and like them. Thus, given the importance of school climate and teacher-student relationships in improving student behavior and academic performance, using rationales is critical to effective teaching.

For some students, a more effective rationale may require focusing on the benefits of behaving appropriately or refraining from inappropriate behavior. Some children, because of their age, developmental level, and a lack of familiarity with a social skills program, are not concerned with how their behavior may affect others. With these students it will be important to identify their individual goals and tailor the rationales to match these goals. This can have a powerful impact on student behavior. For example, if a student is motivated to improve her grades, a teacher can use the rationale that accepting (and implementing) feedback about assignments may help her master the content and receive higher grades on tests or future assignments. For the student whose present goal is to drop out of school as soon as possible, however, such a rationale would not be meaningful. Rather, rationales for staying in school that are related to getting a job after graduation or to daily living issues would be more appropriate.

As mentioned earlier, rationales that emphasize negative consequences are occasionally necessary. For example, pointing out the negative outcomes of fighting may be the most meaningful and direct tie to the behavior. Frequent use of such rationales, however, could make them begin to sound like warnings or threats. Positive rationales usually work better to encourage appropriate behavior.

▶ Components of rationales

Effective rationales are characterized by several elements:

1. They point out natural and logical consequences. Rationales should point out consequences that naturally occur as a result of a behavior. Natural consequences are those that tend to occur without human intervention, or those that are not within the youth's direct control. For example, "If you run down the sidewalk on a rainy day, you could slip and hurt yourself or others," or "If you tip back in your chair, you may fall." Logical consequences, on the other hand, are linked to behavior but are determined more by a student's actions or by others interacting with the student. For example, these rationales state the logical consequences that will result from certain behaviors: "When you greet someone with a smile and say 'Hello,' it may make the person feel good and more likely to want to spend time with you and be your friend"; "If you prepare for a test by studying over a period of time, instead of studying only the night before, you'll probably get a higher grade."

2. They are personal to the youth. Rationales should be geared to the individual interests of each student. This means carefully observing and talking with students to determine their interests, favorite activities, and likes and dislikes. Then, rationales can be specially tailored to each student. For example, if an eighth-grade student enjoys playing basketball and hopes to play on the high school team someday, her teachers can formulate rationales that help the student understand how following instructions or accepting criticism is beneficial. This may include taking criticism from the coach, accepting a referee's decision, or listening to the coach's instructions during practice. Similarly, for a youth whose motivation to graduate is low, rationales that stress the importance of paying attention in classes where he will learn skills that will help him after graduation may be far more effective than talking about higher education.

3. They are specific and brief. Usually, one good rationale is enough to accomplish the purposes of a Teaching Interaction or Effective Praise Interaction. You should be brief and to the point when providing a rationale, and avoid trying to convince the student with numerous reasons. Long explanations may confuse a student; you're more likely to keep a youth's attention with a brief, specific rationale. Even if the tone of the rationale is positive, a lengthy explanation could be perceived as lecturing and punishing. This is especially true for younger students who have shorter attention spans. As the child gets older, it may be more appropriate to get into a more lengthy discussion.

4. They are believable and short-term. Rationales are more effective when immediate consequences are emphasized. For example, an effective rationale for following instructions without arguing might be, "The class may have more free time if you quickly follow instructions and finish your project instead of wasting time arguing." Pointing out this short-term, believable consequence is generally preferable to providing a remote consequence such as, "When you have a job, you will be more likely to get a promotion and a raise if you can follow instructions."

Rationales also must be believable, which means they must be age-appropriate and personalized. For example, you might tell a nine-year-old who enjoys recess, "Putting your things away when I tell you, instead of waiting for the bell to ring, means the class will get to have all of recess time to play." But for a college-bound 17-year-old, a more pertinent rationale may be, "If you study hard and do well on your college entrance exams, you might earn a scholarship, which will make paying for college a lot easier for your parents."

5. They are developmentally appropriate. Rationales that describe short-term, believable consequences are generally the most meaningful for youngsters who are new to a social skills program, or who are less developmentally mature. However, as a youth matures and begins to internalize the gains he or she has made, it also is important to use rationales that point out long-term consequences.

Long-term rationales point out general consequences related to a youngster's behavior – consequences that will occur at some point in the distant future. It is important for youngsters to understand how their behavior may affect their employment, their ability to take care of themselves, and their capacity to develop and maintain relationships. For example, a long-term rationale that could be used when teaching a student how to accept criticism might deal with the youngster's ability in the future to get along with a spouse or keep a job.

Don't forget that other-centered and faith-based reasons need to become important and personal to each student. Rationales about "teamwork," church participation, and working with others are important concepts that aid a young person's development.

It also is critical to encourage students to belong to a parish and participate in youth activities to keep their faith stable, safeguarding their time in Catholic education. Enthusiastically suggest that they take part in the liturgy by being a lector or an EME; perhaps they have already been inspired by seeing you in one of those capacities. As students get closer to graduation, they need, more than ever, to understand that love and concern for others are at the foundation of their faith.

▶ When to use rationales

Rationales can be used whenever teaching occurs. Rationales enhance the teaching of social skills and make learning more relevant and meaningful to a youth by establishing a purpose or reason for the learning.

During the course of a day, there will be numerous informal occasions for you to provide rationales. Students may ask your opinion or you may offer advice or a point of view. Including rationales at every opportunity is extremely helpful.

Briefly, rationales are used in the following contexts:

1. When teaching skills. Rationales should be used in all phases of teaching. When introducing academic concepts or skills, use rationales to establish the relevance of the material to "real-life" situations or future or past learning. When students are told why specific information is being studied, they demonstrate greater understanding and satisfaction about why they should learn what they are asked to learn (Porter & Brophy, 1988). The same can be true for social skills learning.

When you are introducing a new skill, rationales help students understand why they should learn the skill. Rationales that focus on short- and long-term benefits and cover a broad spectrum of situations can be generated by you and the students.

Rationales are extremely important when teaching correctively during a Teaching Interaction. Explaining why a student should change a particular behavior and focusing on the benefits of doing so will help the student realize the cause-effect relationship between the behavior and its outcomes. Understanding this relationship empowers students by helping them learn how to take control of their own behaviors.

2. Whenever disagreements occur between educators and students. Stating why you disagree gives students a chance to "buy into," or at least understand, your point of view. Students also view you as more open-minded and fair. Providing a rationale also models appropriate or desired behavior to students.

3. During problem-solving situations. When you are helping students generate potential solutions to problems, providing rationales helps them evaluate their options. Rationales may help students make better decisions by clarifying the possible benefits or problems associated with each solution.

4. During daily conversations. Students often ask their teachers or other staff members for explanations or advice. Rationales help the student understand the logic behind the explanations or advice.

Although you hope students will understand your rationales and find them meaningful, the goal of using rationales is not to get the students to agree with your reasons. You want students to understand the rationales, but they do not have to agree with your point of view.

Perhaps most importantly, teachers and others working with youth need to remember that rationales alone do not effectively change behavior. Consistently describing behavior and supplying appropriate consequences, coupled with giving good reasons for initiating or maintaining behavior change, will result in the most positive outcomes.

▶ Modeling what you teach

As teachers, the examples we set – how we treat others, how we react to crises, how we praise or listen to or comfort our students – speak as loud as any rationale we can give them for loving God and others. It is not just our actions speaking louder than our words; it shows our students where our hearts are.

If you teach your children to pray, they must see and hear you in prayer. If you tell them to ask God for help or to thank Him for a blessing, they must hear prayers of petition and thanksgiving from your lips.

If you warn your students about the dangers of drinking or gambling and they overhear you talking to another teacher about your "wild weekend," much of your credibility will be lost. If you have a difficult time teaching the Church's position on birth control, your students will very quickly know you don't believe in it. And how can you encourage the reception of the Sacrament of Reconciliation if you don't know Christ's healing touch when you ask for forgiveness?

The Church's doctrine, sacraments, and Scripture are not a multiple-choice issue. They all rely on each other as Christ brings young souls to salvation.

"The human person is present in all the truths of faith: created in 'the image and likeness' of God; elevated by God to the dignity of a child of God; unfaithful to God in original sin, but redeemed by Christ; a temple of the Holy Spirit; a member of the Church; destined to eternal life.

"Students may well object that we are a long way from this ideal. The teacher must listen to these pessimistic responses, but point out that they are also found in the Gospel. Students may need to be convinced that it is better to know the positive picture of personal Christian ethics rather than to get lost in an analysis of human misery. In practice, this means respect for oneself and for others." (The Religious Dimension of Education in a Catholic School, 84)

▶ Summary

There are four main types of rationales: benefits, negative consequences, concern-for-others, and faith-based. Using rationales that are other-centered along with appropriate consequences will produce the optimal conditions for shaping and internalizing appropriate moral standards in students. However, you must decide which type of rationale is best for each student by considering such variables as developmental level, age, personal needs, and the situation at hand. Rationales are used in all the teaching techniques of the Boys Town Education Model, but are extremely helpful in a variety of other formal and informal contacts with students.

By themselves, rationales will not effectively change behavior. They must be paired with specific teaching and appropriate consequences to have the greatest impact.

The greatest challenge confronting teachers in Catholic schools today is becoming articulate about faith issues so they can communicate them to their students. Our classrooms should be laboratories for instructing our children in Christian values. Schools need to be training grounds for developing beliefs that serve Jesus Christ so that children will avoid the tragedy described in Judges 2:10: "...and another generation grew up, who knew neither the Lord nor what He had done...."

Effective praise

"Everything that is good, noble or just – let all this be the object of your thoughts."

Philippians 4:8

Praise is a powerful tool for changing and improving the behaviors of your students. It is crucial to the development of positive relationships between you and your students and is very important in strengthening appropriate behavior. Effective Praise allows you to individualize your teaching of social skills by sincerely and enthusiastically recognizing each student's efforts and progress.

▶ What Is Effective Praise?

Effective Praise is a four-step teaching process that is planned and purposeful. It is specific, genuine, and contingent on positive behavior. Effective Praise should be a totally positive interaction because you are recognizing appropriate behavior and pairing specific descriptions with positive consequences. This means looking carefully for opportunities to praise and reinforce a student's efforts toward positive behavior – to "catch 'em being good." Praising appropriate behavior increases the odds that the desired behavior will occur again.

Steps to Effective Praise

1. Description of appropriate behavior

2. Rationale

3. Request for acknowledgment

4. Positive consequence

Benefits of Effective Praise

Effective Praise helps develop positive relationships between you and your students. Many students have had difficulty developing constructive relationships with adults in authority, or in making or keeping friends. Effective Praise contributes substantially to helping each child learn and grow because you are recognizing the incremental gains being made by each student.

Many students will begin engaging in behaviors that are noticed by others in order to gain approval. Although many of these behaviors may be seen as prosocial by adults, you must guard against developing students who are merely obedient or compliant, and instead work toward developing a sense of responsibility in students. By helping them realize the benefits they will receive, students will begin to develop an internalized set of values and motivation that will result in a sense of personal power (Miller, 1984). Students who act only to please others remain motivated by external factors, have trouble connecting outcomes to their behavior, and may be ill-prepared to function in the changing world (Bluestein, 1988).

A study by Willner, Braukmann, Kirigin, Fixsen, Phillips, and Wolf (1977), found that youth preferred being taught by adults who gave positive feedback, set clear expectations with reasons to back them up, and showed enthusiasm and concern. Similarly, studies have shown that students are more positive and friendly with others in their classrooms and develop more positive "attitudes" when they experience warm and accepting relationships with their teachers (Serow & Soloman, 1979). By design, Effective Praise interactions can meet student needs and facilitate development of relationships.

Effective Praise increases learning and students' behavioral options. As you focus on what a student is doing well, you become more aware of the student's positive behaviors, creating a positive cycle of interactions. The more you're aware of what the student does "right," the more opportunities you have to address and increase positive behavior change. By reinforcing skills that fit societal norms, students increase their repertoire of behavioral responses and begin choosing those that are more readily accepted by others.

How to use Effective Praise

Effective Praise should be used contingently. That is, praise should only be given after a desired behavior occurs, not as a general motivator. By providing praise after a student has demonstrated a particular behavior, you attribute success to the student's effort. This, in turn, implies to the student that similar success can be attained again. It helps students see that they are in charge and in control of their own behavior.

Effective Praise should always specifically describe which behaviors are being recognized and reinforced. Simple, direct statements enhance a student's understanding of what is being praised, and lend credibility to the interaction. Recognizing developmental levels and individual needs when praising students personalizes the inter-actions and shows students you're sincere.

When to use Effective Praise

Use Effective Praise frequently to reinforce new skills. When students are learning something new, they need reinforcement every time they use the skill correctly. Continuous reinforcement builds and strengthens skills. By reinforcing the use of a skill that is just emerging, you increase the likelihood that the student will use the skill again. Skills are developed more quickly, giving students a broader repertoire of appropriate behaviors from which to draw.

Effective Praise also is used when you are attempting to strengthen existing positive behaviors or build the fluency of a skill. As a student demonstrates more frequent and appropriate use of a skill, you should use an intermittent schedule of reinforcement to maintain it. Remember that the "element of surprise," or of not knowing when a behavior will be reinforced, actually increases the chances of the student using the skill. Using an intermittent schedule also helps with fading the use of reinforcers to a more realistic level.

It is important to note that general, nonspecific praise also can be used to maintain a skill. Once the behavior seems well-established, you can begin to fade out the use of specific descriptions until the positive behavior can be sustained through the use of general statements, such as "Good job," "Nice work on the project," and so on. The eventual

goal of Effective Praise is to develop and maintain behavior through social interactions.

Not giving any praise at all may cause the student to stop using the desired behavior. Behavior that was previously reinforced may diminish or cease if it isn't occasionally recognized and addressed. In general, behavior is best maintained when intermittent reinforcement is used.

The steps of Effective Praise

Before discussing the steps of Effective Praise, it is necessary to emphasize an important aspect of this and other interactions you will have with your students. Whenever you talk with students about their behavior, you communicate not only with your words, but also with your actions. **How** you talk with someone is thought to be considerably more important than **what** you actually say. Because of this, you should pay close attention to factors called "quality components." Basically, these components refer to your positive verbal and nonverbal behaviors. They include looking at the student, using a pleasant voice tone, saying the student's name, smiling, using appropriate humor, and showing enthusiasm. Touching, such as a pat on the shoulder, also can be used, but with obvious caution. Of course, your use of touch will be based on many factors and will vary from one student to another.

Quality components establish and maintain a productive climate for learning. In general, everyone is more receptive to teaching when approached positively. You should not only begin any teaching episode with positive behaviors, but also make sure to maintain them throughout the interaction.

You should feel comfortable and natural when using quality components; students will not respond well to an adult who appears insincere or "robotic." When used naturally and spontaneously, quality components can greatly improve the relationships between you and your students.

Here are the steps of Effective Praise:

1. Description of appropriate behavior.

Effective Praise combines specific behavioral statements with your general praise and enthusiasm. Descriptions of appropriate behavior increase the student's level of understanding and the likelihood that he or she will repeat the behavior. These statements help students realize exactly what behaviors fall within the acceptable range. They also help students focus on their accomplishments and progress.

As with any clear description of behavior, describe the circumstances surrounding the behavior – what happened, who was there, when it happened, how it happened, and so on. Again, clear descriptions help teach your youth how to generalize appropriate behavior to similar situations and provide context for your description.

As you make descriptive praise statements, accurately label the skill being taught. For example, "Thanks for looking at me and saying 'Okay' when I asked you to take out your book. You did it right away without bothering others. You did a good job of **following instructions**." Labeling skills

and providing specific behavioral descriptions increase the odds that students will successfully learn new ways of behaving and be able to generalize the skill to future situations.

Specifically describe the skill steps performed correctly by the student. For example, "When I told you that you couldn't use the calculator, **you looked at me, said 'Okay,' and then calmly asked for a reason why**. You did a good job of accepting a 'No' answer."

2. Rationale. Students benefit from learning about the consequences of their behavior. A rationale emphasizes this cause-effect relationship. Realistic, individualized rationales let students know why a specific behavior is beneficial to them or others. To your benefit, students will view you as more concerned and fair. Rationales also can help with compliance – students are more likely to do as they're asked when given a reason for doing so. And finally, rationales increase the pleasantness of interactions and are a key to building relationships with students. For example, "When you accept a 'No' answer like you just did, others will think of you as someone they can work with. Maybe they will try to say 'Yes' to your requests whenever they can."

3. Request acknowledgment. Check to make sure the student is paying attention and understands your rationale by asking for acknowledgment. Although this is a specific step in the sequence, requests for acknowledgment should take place frequently during any teaching. Ask questions such as, "Do you understand?" or "Does that make sense?" or "Do you follow me?" Requesting acknowledgment creates a dialogue; that way, you don't have to lecture.

4. Positive consequence. Positive consequences help promote constructive, rapid behavior change when paired with specific skill teaching. Tell the student what positive consequences were earned for engaging in the specific appropriate behavior. For example, "For doing such a great job of accepting 'No' for an answer, you've earned five extra minutes of independent time," or "You handled that disagreement in your cooperative group so well, you may choose a reading buddy during center time."

In order for the positive consequence to be effective – that is, to strengthen and reinforce the behavior – it must meet several conditions. Rewards need to be individualized. Whereas one student may be reinforced by extra recess time, another student may dislike recess. Also, make sure the size of the reinforcer is appropriate – just large enough to maintain or increase the behavior. Remember, there are many kinds of reinforcers, from tangibles (stickers, marbles, toys), to activities (passing out papers, running an errand, working on the computer), to social reinforcers ("Good job!", a pat on the back, smiles). Use the reinforcer that has demonstrated a positive effect on the student's behavior in the past. Also, refer to Chapter 5, "Principles of Behavior" for more help with reinforcers.

Example 1

Nate is a seventh-grade student in your class. He frequently has difficulty turning assignments in on time, so you have been working with him in this area. Today, Nate turned in his homework from last night and just finished his math assignment with the rest of the class.

1. Description of appropriate behavior: *"Nate, you've really been working hard! First thing this morning, you handed in your homework, and just now you finished your math paper right on time. Great job!"*

2. Rationale: *"Finishing homework and other assignments helps you learn better and faster. By doing assignments on time, you can practice what you just learned and get more of the assignment right because it's fresh in your mind. Then you can move on to the next thing."*

3. Request acknowledgment: *"Do you see why finishing your work on time is important?"*

4. Positive consequence: *"For turning your assignments in on time, you've earned the privilege of being media monitor this afternoon. Way to go!"*

Example 2

Asia is in your second-grade classroom this year. She is most often quiet and shy, participating minimally in class discussions. Today, during opening activities, she shared some information about her baby sister. After opening, when the other children have started their journal entries, you go over to talk with Asia.

1. Description of appropriate behavior: *"Asia, thanks for telling us about your baby sister this morning during opening. You raised your hand, then used a voice that everyone could hear. "*

2. Rationale: *"Sharing in a group can be scary, but it helps others get to know you and gives you things to talk about later, too."*

3. Request acknowledgment: *"See what I mean?"*

4. Positive consequence: *"Since you did such a nice job of sharing in group, you can choose – would you rather hand out our math materials or be first to pick out your computer partner for spelling games?"*

▶ General considerations

Your teaching has the greatest impact when it closely follows a behavior. Relevant, immediate feedback enhances learning. There may be times, however, when you don't observe a positive behavior, but still can praise the student for the choices he or she made. In these cases, you'll need to rely on other sources of information, and talk with the student as soon as you can. For example, another teacher might tell you that she saw one of your students appropriately disagreeing with another student instead of arguing or fighting. In this situation, get as much information as you can, then praise the student for the appropriate behavior.

Most of the time, you will use Effective Praise privately with the student. This provides complete and personal attention. Although occasionally appropriate, public praise can be embarrassing to a student and have counterproductive effects. Public praise probably should be reserved for times when the entire class has demonstrated a skill or when you know a particular student will respond positively.

Effective Praise does not replace your use of general praise. It is intended as a teaching tool and doesn't need to be employed every time a student does something well. Tailor the type and frequency of your teaching to suit each child's particular needs.

Positive interactions with students, including Effective Praise, should occur at least four times as often as you use corrective interactions. This 4:1 ratio enhances relationships, results in more positive behavior from your students, and helps build "reinforcement reserves" for students. Frequently telling students what they are doing well helps them focus on their positive behaviors. This can help them feel more competent and better about themselves. When Corrective Teaching does occur, students have both emotional and token reinforcement reserves to fall back on. The 4:1 ratio is a minimum standard; many children need higher ratios of positive-to-corrective feedback to show improvement.

▶ Summary

Effective Praise is a four-step planned teaching process that is used to recognize and reward a student's appropriate behavior. The way you use Effective Praise is very important. When given in a manner that is direct, personal, specific, and pleasant, it will seem natural and sincere. Noticing what each student does well will show that you are sensitive and responsive to the needs of all your students. Perhaps more importantly, your students will feel better about themselves and will be encouraged to work even harder in the positive, caring educational atmosphere you have created.

Preventive teaching

New teachers often worry about whether they will be able to control their students' behavior. They hope that most children have received a gradual education on how to behave from their parents and other adults through modeling, discussions, praise, and discipline. Unfortunately, many students today have not been a part of such a natural process. In fact, they often have had inconsistent or dysfunctional models who have left them confused and socially unskilled. Teachers who effectively use Preventive Teaching, along with other consistent teaching techniques, can help these youngsters make up for skill deficits.

▶ Classroom management and Preventive Teaching

A synthesis of considerable research (Northwest Regional Education Laboratory, 1990) revealed strong evidence that when effective classroom strategies are employed, student behavior, attitudes, and achievement improve measurably. Two key elements of good management cited in the report are establishing and maintaining consistent expectations and developing positive teacher-student relationships. These factors have been found to be far more effective as classroom management techniques than those which seek to maintain control by focusing solely or primarily on student misbehavior. Unfortunately, teachers often tend to notice and deal with disruptive behavior as a way to maintain order in the classroom. The methods used to do this can have a significant negative effect on students. Jones and Jones (1981), for example, found that negative remarks by teachers are correlated with student dislike for school. Similarly, Becker, Engelmann, and Thomas (1975) reported that critical remarks by teachers tend to worsen student behavior rather than improve it.

More-successful approaches to classroom management involve techniques designed to prevent problems before they occur (Kounin, 1970). Kounin found that one way to minimize student disruption was to maximize the time spent in active learning. Addressing and resolving minor incidents before they became major problems decreased time spent on disruptive behavior. Kounin found that teachers can achieve more effective classroom management by:

1. Watching classroom activity at all times. Effective managers station themselves so they can scan the entire classroom and see each student. This enables them to spot and deal with minor problems before they become serious or disruptive. This form of monitoring also communicates to students that the teacher is very aware of what is occurring in the classroom at all times.

2. Performing several tasks at once. Effective managers can lead a group discussion, take care of "housekeeping" activities such as attendance, or engage students in small group activities while also monitoring and addressing student behavior.

3. Being prepared to teach. This allows teachers to maintain a brisk pace and avoid lapses because they need to check a manual or scan notes to see what to do next. Effective managers also maintain the "academic flow" by dealing with inattention without disrupting the class. Common techniques include establishing eye contact, asking the student a question pertaining to the subject, or regaining attention with a comment to the student.

Using direct classroom observations, Anderson, Evertson, and Emmer (1980) expanded on Kounin's original research and found that classrooms ran smoother when teachers demonstrated these key behaviors and set expectations at the beginning of the school year. Teachers experiencing the most success spent quite a bit of time on classroom rules and procedures during the first few weeks of school, introducing them gradually to avoid overloading students with too much information. Effective managers went beyond merely informing students of rules and expectations. In short, they taught rules and procedures in the same manner as academic subjects – through modeling, discussion, practice, and feedback on performance. Additionally, consequences for appropriate and inappropriate behaviors were consistently applied.

▶ Preventive Teaching in society

Practical applications of Preventive Teaching can be found in a variety of social and daily living contexts. Preventive Teaching is used whenever particular skills or behaviors need to be learned to handle specific situations. For example, in fire drills, occupants of a building locate alarms and extinguishers, and practice using exit routes in order to help reduce the chances of serious injury in a fire. To prepare their children to walk to school, parents may schedule a practice walk in which they show the route to school, where and how to cross streets, and where to find "block homes" a child can go to for help if necessary. We teach children how to dial the "911" emergency number to report an accident, injury, or threatening situation, and provide them with rules about dealing with strangers. On-the-job training programs provide instruction in dealing with difficult customers, handling hazardous materials, using new equipment, and many other topics to prepare employees for situations they may face. By reviewing and practicing specific behaviors that match particular situations in advance, greater success can be expected when the actual situation is encountered.

▶ Benefits of Preventive Teaching

In addition to the general benefit of improving classroom management, as described earlier in this chapter, Preventive Teaching provides many specific benefits to students and teachers.

1. Preventive Teaching enhances the effectiveness of teachers. From the start, teachers can set clear expectations for student behavior. Through "up-front" teaching, you are able to establish and demonstrate tolerance levels and consequences. You are able to model these expectations as you teach skills, and communicate the importance of skill-building through repeated instruction and feedback to students. You also can keep a strong focus on individual goals for students, knowing that expectations may vary from student to student.

2. Preventive Teaching increases the opportunities for student learning. Because students are actively involved in Preventive Teaching lessons, their chances of acquiring skills are improved. Gaining their input,

having them practice skills in "safe" situations, and allowing them to give positive feedback to others keep students involved in the learning process. They may acquire skills more quickly because lessons are presented at a neutral time – that is, in the absence of interfering behavior – which may help them be more open to feedback on their performance.

3. Preventive Teaching builds relationships and increases comfort levels. The entire Preventive Teaching process demonstrates respect, concern and fairness. It allows students to learn and practice skills at a neutral time, thereby providing a nonthreatening, positive atmosphere. The use of positive consequences demonstrates recognition of the students' efforts and communicates the importance of the skills you are working on. Teachers often report feeling more confident and comfortable when their students are placed in situations that may be new, different, or have the potential to affect others (e.g., an assembly, field trip, or guest speaker). The time invested in skill development can pay off with greater student self-confidence and less stress for the teacher.

▶ When to use Preventive Teaching

Preventive Teaching can be used to focus on basic or advanced social skills, to prepare students for specific situations or circumstances, and to individualize social skills teaching to fit the needs of individual students. Although the most logical time to use Preventive Teaching may seem like the beginning of each school year when you establish classroom rules, it can and should be used whenever a need is identified.

Perhaps your first opportunity to use Preventive Teaching is when you introduce the Boys Town Social Skills Curriculum. You should plan to spend some time talking about social skills – what they are, how you will teach them to students, why they are important, and the students' responsibilities for using them. You'll also use Preventive Teaching to talk to your students about other components of the overall program, such as Teaching Interactions, consequences, and office referrals.

The beginning of the school year is an ideal time to use Preventive Teaching to establish classroom rules and expectations. You can help your students "buy in" by making sure they are actively involved in creating the rules and guidelines.

You should plan to use Preventive Teaching whenever the need arises during the course of the school year. Special events or situations, individual needs of students, identification of weak skills for the entire class, and the entry of a new student all suggest the use of Preventive Teaching.

Preventive Teaching can be used with individual students, small groups, or the whole class. While individualized Preventive Teaching typically focuses on a student's particular areas of need, group instruction is geared toward skills that all students need to know. Group lessons can be related to academic content or concepts, such as safe use of science lab equipment or types of punctuation, or to behavioral expectations like how to introduce oneself or how to act at an assembly. Group teaching allows you to efficiently teach necessary skills and to interact positively with students.

▶ Preventive Teaching sequences

Preventive Teaching comprises three stages: Planned Teaching, Preteaching, and Preventive Prompt. Planned Teaching is used to introduce a new skill to students at a planned, neutral time. Preteaching is used to reintroduce a skill prior to a specific event or situation in which the student will need to use the skill. A Preventive Prompt is a brief reminder to the student about the skill immediately before the event or situation occurs.

Planned Teaching

Planned Teaching is a systematic introduction of a new skill to a student or group of students at a planned, neutral time. Planned Teaching should be used frequently, especially with new students, to help them learn and practice the social skills. The steps of a Planned Teaching sequence are shown below.

Planned Teaching sequence (Stage I)

1. Introduce skill
2. Describe appropriate behavior
3. Give rationale
4. Request acknowledgment
5. Practice
6. Feedback
7. Positive consequence
8. Future/follow-up practice

1. Introduce skill. To begin the Planned Teaching sequence, label the skill to be taught and carefully describe situations in which the skill may be used. A number of specific examples should be provided and students should have opportunities to contribute and ask questions. By describing the skill in a variety of contexts, you'll help students generalize the application of the skill to a variety of antecedent conditions or settings. A demonstration of the skill also may be an effective teaching tool during the introduction.

Example: *"Today, we're going to talk about a skill called 'Introducing Yourself.' Everybody think about a time when you introduced yourself to someone. Be ready to share about that time."*

2. Describe appropriate behavior. Following the general explanation, you should specifically describe each step of the skill. In cases where you're teaching a set of behaviors that does not appear on the 16-skill curriculum list, analyze the overall behavior (e.g., "staying on task") into observable components and teach each step. Make sure you clearly state your expectations or criterion levels to achieve the best results. You may need to spend time defining terms, discussing exceptions or special circumstances, and teaching specific behaviors that make up some of your steps (See Chapter 6, "Teaching the Curriculum Skills.")

Example: *"Here are the steps for 'Introducing Yourself.' Let's talk about shaking someone's hand. When do you think you would or wouldn't do that? What else might you do, instead? What would you do if the other person didn't extend his or her hand?"*

3. Give Rationale. List a variety of benefits or payoffs that may be derived from using the new skill. Students should be involved in generating rationales to enhance meaning and ownership.

Example: *"Think about why it could be important to introduce yourself in the way we just talked about. Be ready to share your ideas."*

4. Request acknowledgment. Including this step allows you to determine whether students understand why or how using a skill can be beneficial to them. Students don't have to agree with every rationale provided, but should acknowledge that they can understand the benefits involved. A second part of this step is to have students repeat the skill steps to you. Requesting group responses, mixed with randomly calling on individual students, may be an effective way to increase participation and attention. Depending on the skill levels of the students, you may want to use verbal or visual cues to prompt responses.

Example: *"Can everyone see why it may be important to introduce yourself like we've talked about? Give me a 'thumbs up' if that makes sense."* (Part 1)

"Everybody think about the first step of the skill. Look at me when you know what it is. Tell us the first step, Michelle." (Part 2)

5. Practice. This step actively involves students in brief role-plays and demonstrations. During the practice, you can monitor the students' progress and adjust your teaching, as needed. You should maximize the time spent in practice by including a variety of activities. Paired practice, in which students work with a partner, provides a chance for everyone to participate. Small groups can be equally effective and provide an opportunity for students to work on cooperative skills, as well. You should be actively involved during the practice by closely observing and monitoring group interactions.

Student-to-teacher practices can be used when teaching individual student groups. You may ask for volunteers to demonstrate the skill with you as the class observes and prepares to give positive feedback. Since the greatest amount of learning takes place by doing, you should plan to allow an adequate amount of time on this step.

Example: *"Turn to your partner and practice the steps of 'Introducing Yourself.' I'll be watching for all the steps we discussed."*

6. Feedback. Specific, descriptive feedback should follow the practice(s). If the lesson was structured well, most of your feedback should be positive, but there also may be opportunities for corrective feedback. Generally, the feedback should be given by the teacher or instructor to ensure its appropriateness.

Example: *"Great! I saw lots of smiles and head nods, and heard nice voice tones and words like 'Nice to meet you.' I even saw lots of you shake hands with your partner."*

7. Positive consequence. Planned Teaching always includes a positive consequence for positive behaviors exhibited by your students. Consequences should be varied, ranging from a pat on the back to extra recess or homework passes. Determining consequences is generally easy when working with an individual student, but somewhat more

difficult when teaching a large group. Group consequences must be carefully selected to make sure the reinforcement is contingent upon everyone's performance. Group behaviors you may be able to reinforce include participating, staying on task, making positive comments, and practicing the skill. Individual efforts also should be recognized by privately discussing appropriate behaviors with the particular student(s). For example, a student who volunteered to demonstrate or practice the skill in front of the class may receive an additional positive consequence for volunteering.

Example: *"Everyone did so well practicing the skill and participating in the lesson, you've earned three minutes of quiet visiting time with your neighbor."*

8. Future/follow-up practice. To close the Planned Teaching sequence, tell the student(s) about the next opportunity for practicing the skill with you. Establish exactly when the next rehearsal or review will occur to help students understand the importance of the lesson. Follow-up sessions will reinforce your initial teaching efforts by allowing additional exposure to the skill during neutral times. To increase generalization, you may assign homework or other activities (See "Teaching for Generalization," later in this chapter).

Example: *"Tomorrow, right after opening activities, we'll again talk about 'Introducing Yourself.'"*

Preteaching

Preteaching is the second stage of Preventive Teaching. During the Preteaching sequence, the skill is reintroduced prior to a specific situation in which the student needs to use the skill. Preteaching reinforces concepts presented in the original Planned Teaching sequence and prepares students to handle a specific, upcoming situation. Here is the Preteaching sequence:

Preteaching sequence (Stage II)

1. Reintroduce skill

2. Describe appropriate behavior

3. Rationale

4. Request acknowledgment

5. Practice (optional)

6. Feedback

7. Positive consequence

8. Inform student of upcoming situation

The Preteaching sequence is similar to the Planned Teaching sequence, but because many of the concepts are being reintroduced, it may not take as much time. Students should be more involved in the Preteaching sequence, providing descriptions of appropriate behavior (i.e., skill steps) and rationales. The practice portion of the Preteaching sequence is optional; the decision to practice depends upon the student's needs, including how well the student remembers and understands the skill being taught. Feedback should, again, be positive and specific, and corrective, if needed. Students will earn a positive consequence for participating in a Preteaching sequence, as they did during Planned Teaching.

Finally, students should be informed of a specific, upcoming situation in which they'll need to use the skill they've been practicing. For example, they may be asked to introduce themselves to a new student who will be enrolling in your class the following day. Or you may inform them that the school will be having a fire drill sometime within the next few days, and that they'll need to demonstrate their skills of quickly and quietly exiting the classroom and building. If the skill you've been teaching can be used in a variety of situations (e.g., accepting criticism, following instructions), you may inform students that you'll be planning different situations in which they can practice the skill they've been learning.

Preventive Prompt

The last stage of Preventive Teaching is a Preventive Prompt. The prompt is a brief reminder or statement about the use of a skill just prior to the event or situation in which a student will use it. Examples of Preventive Prompts include asking a student, "Do you remember the steps to following instructions?", just before instructing the student to clean the blackboard, or saying, "Remember the steps we talked about for leaving the building during a fire drill" as the alarm begins to sound. Additionally, prompts should not be used "after the fact." A Preventive Prompt is not intended to remind students about what they should have done after you've observed inappropriate behavior. For example, after a student has failed to follow a particular instruction you've given, you should not respond by saying "Now, remember what we've been saying about how to follow instructions?"

The eventual goal is that you will be able to fade prompts and that students will automatically use skills in response to various situations or stimuli. Through repeated guided practice, students learn new responses to situations and begin to substitute skill-based behaviors for old behavioral patterns.

▶ Teaching for generalization

While the entire Preventive Teaching process aids with generalization, some of the steps are geared even more specifically to promoting the use of social skills in other situations. Of the steps, rationales most directly help students understand potential positive outcomes in various applications. The practice step helps students "overlearn" a skill which may, then, transfer to novel situations.

Other generalization techniques which easily fit the education setting, as discussed in Dowd and Tierney (1992), include:

1. Training in different settings. The actual training setting should resemble, as closely as possible, situations the student is likely to encounter. Since many of our lessons are intended to carry over to classroom or other school-related situations, this facet of instruction should be fairly easy to achieve. You may increase the "realism" of your instruction by having students practice skills in actual contexts, as appropriate. For example, if you are teaching lunchroom or assembly behavior, taking your students to those areas of the building to practice skills could facilitate transfer.

2. Training with different people. Students may generalize skills more easily and quickly if they receive instruction from different people. Whenever possible, include people who will be directly involved with your students in different contexts. Having the playground aide, your "team teacher," or a counselor participate in practices for situations which routinely involve them will enhance transfer.

3. "Homework" assignments. Like academics, the use of social skills homework can help students retain and generalize new information. You may ask students to try out a particular social skill with a friend, family member, or other adult, then record the result and be prepared to report outcomes during the next session.

▶ Summary

Preventive Teaching builds relationships and fosters skill development. It can be used to teach basic and advanced curriculum skills and to prepare students for specific situations or circumstances. Preventive Teaching can be used effectively with individual students, small groups, or an entire class. Consistent use of Preventive Teaching can decrease the seriousness and frequency of problem behaviors in the classroom by helping students systematically learn new patterns of behavior.

The teaching interaction

The Teaching Interaction is a nine-step process used to address inappropriate social behaviors and teach prosocial alternatives. Consistent use of the Teaching Interaction allows you to effectively meet the individual needs of each student. Teaching Interactions also help you build and maintain relationships with your students. By teaching alternative behaviors in a calm and pleasant manner, you show your concern for students and enhance the effectiveness of your teaching.

▶ When to use the Teaching Interaction

When a student behaves inappropriately, you should use a Teaching Interaction to teach a new skill or strengthen a weak skill. Your primary goal is to teach alternative, replacement behaviors and reduce or eliminate inappropriate ones. Rather than suppressing inappropriate behavior, you focus on building self-management skills so students can make better choices about how they act. Consistent teaching, including opportunities to practice a new skill, makes learning more efficient because the time you spend addressing behavior is productive and relevant.

Simply addressing inappropriate behavior as it happens will not, by itself, promote positive change. To build and maintain prosocial behavior, you must reinforce students' efforts to use appropriate behavior at least four times as often as you address their mistakes. Frequent reinforcement lets students know you notice what they do well and increases the likelihood of the behavior reoccurring. (See Chapter 9, "Effective Praise.")

▶ Teaching Interaction components

The nine steps of the Teaching Interaction can, over time, help students learn better responses to potential problems. Corrective Teaching occurs in an atmosphere of genuine concern for students (Dowd & Tierney, 1992).

The Teaching Interaction

1. Initial praise or empathy

2. Description of inappropriate behavior

3. Description of appropriate behavior

4. Rationale

5. Request for acknowledgment

6. Practice

7. Feedback

8. Consequences

9. General praise/Redirection

When you approach a student to discuss an inappropriate behavior, it is important to be conscious of your behavior. Even though your focus is on correction of a mistake, you want to convey care and concern through your general tone and nonverbal behaviors. Thus, your teaching should always be accompanied by positive quality components. These include looking at the student, using a pleasant voice tone, calling the student by name, and having a pleasant or neu-tral facial expression. To make your teaching personal and to maintain the student's dignity, quietly address his or her behavior, within a reasonably close proximity and on the same physical plane. Used throughout your teaching, these components increase student receptivity to feedback and help you maintain a positive tone.

Initial praise or empathy

The interaction begins with a positive statement related to the behavior you are teaching. Your praise will appear much more genuine if it is related to the teaching situation. For example, Desiree wants your attention. She waves her arm in the air and calls out loudly, "I need some help over here!" You could praise her for a number of behaviors: staying in her seat, raising her hand, asking for help, staying on task, looking at you. In another situation, you greet Dan as he enters the classroom. He looks away from you, rolls his eyes, and walks by you without saying anything. Although it appears that there were no behaviors that warrant praise, you could still praise Dan for getting to class on time that day or going promptly to his seat.

Initial praise reinforces approximations of the desired behavior and helps the student recognize progress. It enhances your relationships with students by showing them that you are aware of their accomplishments, even when they display inappropriate behaviors. Also, by focusing on something the student did well, you start the interaction on a positive note and are less likely to be seen as negative or punishing.

You also may choose to begin your interaction with an empathy statement to let the student know that you understand what he or she is experiencing. Like praise, empathy helps set a positive tone and makes students more receptive to your correction. Using Desiree's situation as an example, you may empathize with her needing your help by saying, "I can understand that you'd really like some help with your assignment." You may find that older students respond better to empathy than praise, as it may seem more genuine and less contrived.

Without the consistent use of this step, students may come to view you as punishing — someone who is quick to criticize mistakes and slow to recognize accomplishments. If this happens, students may begin to actively avoid you because you represent negative consequences to them.

Description of inappropriate behavior

Specifically describe to the student his or her inappropriate behavior. Using objective, behavioral terms, and describe antecedent events and student actions to structure your teaching. For example, in the earlier situation with Dan, you might say, "When you came in this morning and I said 'Hello,' you looked away and rushed past me without saying anything." This description "sets the stage" for your teaching by clearly telling the student what he did and helping you decide what skill to teach.

Avoid using judgmental terms in your descriptions. Describe behaviors instead of perceived intent or motive. For example,

instead of telling a student, "Why are you being so disrespectful to Sue? You were just trying to hurt her feelings, weren't you?", focus on the specific behaviors. Use a statement such as, "When you passed by Sue's desk, you told her she was a slob and then laughed at her." (See Chapter 7, "Observing and Describing Behavior," for a complete discussion of these concepts.)

Keep your descriptions brief and to the point in order to avoid badgering the student. Focus on the most overt or obvious behaviors, then move on. The purpose of this step is to increase the student's awareness of the behavior, so you can shift the emphasis to providing appropriate alternatives.

Description of appropriate behavior

Following the description of the inappropriate behavior, teach the student an appropriate alternative behavior. This description not only helps the student understand your expectations, but also assists him or her in learning social skills that can be used in other settings. To promote this generalization, use words like, "A better way to greet someone...," or "Whenever someone gives you feedback...." Using this phrasing, rather than "I" statements such as "I'd like you to," focuses the student on self-management skills instead of teacher-pleasing behavior.

As part of your description, label the skill so the teaching will be clear for you and the student. Teach each of the incremental behaviors that comprise the skill. For example, "A better way to greet people is to look at them, smile, use a pleasant voice tone, and say something like 'Good morning.'" If necessary, you can demonstrate or model the behaviors in order to make the description clear for the student. (See Chapter 6, "The Social Skills Curriculum.")

Rationale

Offering the student a rationale after the description of the appropriate behavior tells him or her why the skill should be learned and used. The rationale should be personal, skill-based, and brief, and should explain the short-term benefits the student can receive by using the skill. This helps the student internalize the behavior. Your rationale may explain the benefits of using a skill, negative outcomes of not using the skill, or how the student's behavior affects others. (See Chapter 8, "Rationales.")

Rationales help students understand the link between their behavior and possible outcomes. This helps them learn to take responsibility for their behaviors, rather than blaming outside forces for what happens to them. It also empowers students to understand that their behavioral choices, in part, determine what may happen to them. For example, you may tell a student who is learning how to greet others and is interested in making friends, "If you say 'Hi' to people in the hall, it may help you start a conversation with them and they may want to get to know you better."

Request for acknowledgment

Requests for acknowledgment should occur throughout the teaching process to gauge student comprehension and to pro-mote student participation. This component follows the rationale so that you can determine whether the student understands the rationale. Questions like, "Does that make sense?" and "Do you understand?" are effective at determining student responsiveness. Avoid asking the student questions like, "Do you agree?" or "How do you feel about that?" These types of questions can lead to the student arguing with you. The important point here is not that the student agrees with you, but that he or she understands what you are saying.

It also is a good idea to have the student repeat the skill's steps before practicing. This is most beneficial for students who are just learning the skill, or students who have had repeated difficulties with certain behaviors. Rather than asking a question like, "Could you tell me the steps for greeting someone?" and risk getting a "No" answer, say something like, "Tell me how you're going to greet people now," or "Tell me the steps for greeting others."

Practice

Having the student practice the alternative behavior provides an opportunity to immediately use the skill in a "low-risk" situation. Just as practice helps a student learn an academic concept, the practice step acts as a bridge between the initial inappropriate behavior and progress toward skill proficiency. The student's performance during the practice also gives you an idea of how well you taught the skill. This is the only time during the Teaching Interaction where you can assess your teaching effectiveness and determine whether reteaching is necessary.

In order for the practice to be most effective, set it up very clearly for the student. The student should know exactly what he or she is supposed to do, what skill is being practiced, and what you are going to do. For example, in setting up a practice for greeting someone, you might say, "Dan, here's an opportunity to use greeting skills just like we talked about. This time, you'll look at me, smile, and in a pleasant voice tone say 'Good morning.'" Ask the student if he or she understands your instructions so the student knows what to do. Say something like, "Does that make sense?" Then give the student a cue to begin the practice to separate your setup from the actual practice.

Usually, the student will practice the skill in the original context. That is, if the student had trouble accepting criticism about a term paper, you'd give him or her the same criticism in the practice. If the original situation was somewhat "heated," you should make sure to prompt the student that you'll practice the same situation again. This helps you avoid any of the difficulties the student had with the original situation, brings closure to the episode, and ensures a greater transfer of learning.

Practice sessions can sometimes be more successful and helpful to the student if you use a similar but hypothetical situation. This is especially true if the original issue involved a very emotional or intense response by the student, or if it was disruptive to your class. If so, you may choose to teach the same skill in a different context. For example, Darla is out of her seat looking out the window. You give her an instruction to sit down, but she remains standing for quite some time before going back to her seat. Now, when you teach the skill of "Following Instructions," it would distract the class and Darla if you sent her back to the window during the practice. Instead, you could have her practice following another instruction, such as getting started on her assignment, opening her book to a certain page, or taking out necessary supplies for the class. All these instructions would lead Darla toward being back on task with the rest of the class. Similarly, if the original situation involved an intense student reaction, you may choose to practice the skill in a pretend situation first. After a successful practice, you then could return to the actual situation for a final practice of the skill.

Some practices will have to be done later, at a more suitable time. For example, a student who comes into class late may have to practice being on time after class or when she returns to your class the next day. In any practice situation, if the student doesn't achieve predetermined criteria, he or she should practice again. Most of the time, the student will practice the entire skill as you have described it. However, for students who are just learning skills, you may be looking for only a few steps at a time. These students are in the "shaping" process; they require praise for approximations of the desired behaviors.

Feedback

Following the practice, provide the student with positive feedback about his or her performance that includes specific descriptions of the student's behavior. Depending on the student's original behavior and skill level, your specific description of the practice could include anything from a verbal replay to selected highlights. For example, Malcolm has been working on the skill of "Making a Request" for some time. Although he has learned most of the steps, he often forgets to say "Thank-you." When he successfully practices the skill using all the steps, your feedback might be, "Great request! This time you remembered to say 'Thank you.'" If another practice is necessary, praise the student for any approximations of the behavior before asking him or her to practice again.

Praise and descriptive feedback will increase the likelihood that students will engage in appropriate behaviors again. Your feedback also demonstrates concern, shows support for students' progress, and reinforces appropriate behavior. Finally, it contributes to and helps build relationships between you and your students.

Consequences (response cost and positive correction)

For engaging in an inappropriate behavior, the student should earn a negative consequence (response cost). In other words, he loses something that is reinforcing to him. The negative consequence serves to deter the student from engaging in that behavior in the future. For further illustration of this concept, see Chapter 5, "Principles of Behavior."

When issuing negative consequences, you will want to consider the following:

Size. Consider how large the consequence has to be in order to be effective. Start small, using the least amount of "response cost" possible to produce the greatest change. When deciding the size of the consequence, consider the frequency with which the behavior occurs, and its severity. A frequent or severe behavior would obviously warrant a heavier consequence.

Difficulty. Also consider the difficulty the student has in performing the appropriate alternative behavior. If the student is very deficient in the skill of "Following Instructions," for example, he will probably need many opportunities to practice the skill during the course of the school day, and many opportunities to make mistakes. If his teacher were to issue a large consequence every time the student did not follow instructions, the student would be buried in penalties by mid-morning, and have little incentive to work on using the skill.

Appropriateness of the consequence. Like rewards, negative consequences need to be individualized to ensure that they are indeed effective. To determine the effectiveness of a response cost, look at the behavioral outcome. That is, if the behavior diminishes or stops, the consequence was effective; if the behavior continues or gets worse, it was not. For example, Theo loves playing soccer with his friends at recess. When he has difficulty staying on-task during class, he loses 10 minutes of his recess so that he can practice the skill and finish his work. Losing 10 minutes of soccer time is enough of a consequence to help Theo stay on task the following day.

In addition to the negative consequence of a response cost, the Boys Town Education Model also offers praise and/or positive correction for practicing the alternative appropriate behavior. That is, the student loses something reinforcing, but because he practiced the skill during the Teaching Interaction, he "earns back" part of what he lost. This combination helps motivate students to change their behaviors and to cooperate during your teaching. It also allows you to reinforce the student for correcting his behavior and engaging in appropriate alternative behavior.

When issuing negative consequences in the Teaching Interaction, keep in mind that consequences should be viewed as if on a continuum, starting with the least-restrictive consequence that will promote the greatest behavior change. The least restrictive consequence is the Teaching Interaction itself. The student loses some of his time as you address his behavior and have him practice the alternative. With Dan, for example, issuing the consequence may sound like this:

"Because you had trouble greeting me this morning, we had to take a little time and discuss a better way to greet people, and then practice that skill. But you did a nice practice, so why don't you take your seat and we'll get started."

Many students have difficulty seeing the connection between their behavior and the natural consequences that ensue. In addition to the Teaching Interaction as a consequence, you may also want to point out to students what occurred naturally as a result of their behavior. For example, when Darnell yells out to get his teacher's help, he doesn't get the help he wants as quickly as he desires. But by practicing, he can get her assistance and the help he needs. His consequence may sound like this:

"Because you had a hard time getting my attention, you still haven't gotten your question answered. But since you practiced, I can answer it now and give you the help you need."

When behavior becomes more severe or more frequent, as previously mentioned, the size of the consequence should fit the severity or frequency of the behavior. Still, your consequence should be a logical response cost. For example, when Troy fights on the playground, he has to stand by the teacher for the remainder of recess. For practicing the alternative behavior (ignoring peers, taking turns, etc.), he earns back some of that time. Because Christy is repeatedly off-task, she is unable to finish her work and must stay after school and finish it while she practices the skill of staying on task.

Some situations call for compensatory behavior and/or restitution, another logical consequence. When Bo gets into a fight with a classmate, he has to apologize and do something nice for the other student. For behavior that is severe or becoming patternistic, you may want to contact parents to set up a conference to discuss possible interventions.

General praise/Redirection

This step is as much for you as it is for the student. It is designed to positively redirect the student and end the interaction on a positive note. Rather than summarizing the interaction, simple and brief praise like "Nice job" or "Good work" is the most natural way to end your teaching. Any further mention of the student's behavior, even when stated in a positive manner, may serve to undermine your efforts. Statements such as, "Now I know you'll be able to follow instructions" or "I'm sure you won't make the same mistake next time" can communicate unrealistic expectations, setting students up for failure.

▶ Sample Teaching Interaction

Dan is a fourth-grade student. As he enters your classroom one morning, and you greet him, he looks away from you and says nothing as he rushes past. As the rest of the class visits quietly before the bell rings, you approach Dan at his desk to talk with him about his greeting.

Initial praise or empathy: *"Dan, I'm glad you made it to school this morning and I appreciate you looking up just now."*

Description of inappropriate behavior: *"When I greeted you a moment ago, you rushed past me, and didn't say anything."*

Description of appropriate behavior: *"Whenever someone greets you, whether it's a teacher or other kids at school, it would be better if you would look at the person, smile, use a pleasant voice, and say something like 'Hello.'"*

Rationale: *"Dan, when you greet people like that, they're more likely to see you as friendly and want to get to know you better. You could even end up with more friends."*

Request for acknowledgment: *"Do you understand what I'm saying?* (Dan says, "Uh-huh.") *Okay, tell me the steps for greeting others."* (Dan gives all the steps of the skill.)

Practice: *"Good job, Dan. Let's try that greeting again. This time, I want you to greet me by using all those steps. We'll just pretend we're standing at the door like before."* (Dan successfully practices the skill.)

Feedback: *"Excellent! This time you looked right at me, smiled, and pleasantly said 'Hello.'*

Consequences: *"Initially, Dan, you had some trouble greeting me, and we had to take some time this morning and talk about a better way to greet others. Because of that, you missed out on some visiting time with your friends. But you did a nice job practicing the skill with me. And, you still have some time left to go talk with your friends."*

General praise/Redirection: *"Thanks Dan, you did a really nice job listening to me. After the bell rings, let's start working on your vocabulary review."*

▶ General considerations

Throughout the interaction, you should recognize and praise appropriate behaviors, particularly those that have been difficult for the student in the past. When you notice and praise these behaviors, students are more likely to continue to be responsive to your feedback.

When you notice mild inattentive behaviors before or during a Teaching Interaction, give a brief prompt to get the student's attention. Teaching social skills, like academics, is not effective when the student is inattentive. For example, you could say, "Edwin, could you put your book down and look at me, please? Thanks." If the behavior continues, escalates, or reoccurs frequently, you should use techniques described in Chapter 12, "Ongoing Behavior."

Just as consequences should be viewed on a continuum, there should be a continuum of interventions when dealing with an inappropriate student behavior. It would be impossible, as well as unnecessary, to do a nine-step Teaching Interaction following every inappropriate student behavior. Initially prompting the inappropriate behavior is the least-restrictive intervention. Make your prompts as instructional as possible so as to prevent further intervention.

Example: *"Instead of yelling, James, you should raise your hand and wait for me to call on you."*

"Remember to say 'Please' when you ask for something, Terence."

If the inappropriate behavior diminishes or stops, then you know the prompt was effective. When the behavior becomes more severe or more frequent, your prompt was ineffective and a Teaching Interaction may be necessary. Always remember, however, to recognize and reinforce the student for engaging in the prosocial alternative behavior at least four times as often as you teach or attend to the inappropriate behavior to help the student make the behavior part of his repertoire.

And finally, the ultimate goal of using the Teaching Interaction is to give your students a cognitive tool for self-management. Initially, you will guide them through the steps of the Teaching Interaction by helping them identify more appropriate alternative behaviors. Eventually, your students will incorporate what you have taught and be able to correct their social errors on their own, while learning new prosocial behaviors.

▶ Summary

The Teaching Interaction is a flexible tool that can be adapted to meet students' varying needs. By modifying your language and adjusting the expectations for the student, you can successfully use the Teaching Interaction with students of all ages and skill levels.

CHAPTER TWELVE

Ongoing behavior

Teaching Interactions are used when a student engages in inappropriate behaviors. However, nearly all students will at times have trouble accepting your feedback while they are being corrected and will display behaviors that interfere with your teaching. This is called **ongoing behavior**, and is defined as inattentive or problem behavior that occurs during a Teaching Interaction and interferes with the student's ability to learn.

Dealing with ongoing behavior when it occurs benefits both you and the student. Rather than responding emotionally, you should view these behaviors as skill deficits and as opportunities to teach students better ways to manage their behavior when faced with criticism. You will be better able to deal with ongoing behavior calmly and objectively once you "depersonalize" it by viewing it as a "teachable moment."

When a student begins to show signs of not accepting correction during a Teaching Interaction, it will be necessary to temporarily stop the interaction. You can't "teach over" the interfering behaviors during social skills instruction any more than you can when teaching a critical academic concept. Both require student attentiveness and responsiveness. Instead, you'll use techniques (explained later in this chapter) that are designed to help the student regain self-control before you continue teaching.

Ongoing behavior can take many forms, ranging from subtle to overt. Some examples include:

Facial expressions – looking away, glaring, rolling the eyes, frowning, and grinning.

Verbal behaviors – interrupting, arguing, swearing, talking to others, and mumbling.

Body movements – slouching, folding arms, turning and/or walking away, moving excessively, making noise with hands or other objects, gestures with fingers or hands, and resting one's head on a desk or hand.

Other behaviors – not answering when asked to respond, sighing, crying, and laughing.

Ongoing behaviors are the opposite of attentive behaviors, which generally include looking at you, responding to questions or instructions, sitting or standing quietly, and maintaining a neutral facial expression. Your expectations for each student engaging in these attentive behaviors will depend largely on the student's developmental level and his or her current level of skill acquisition.

▶ Preventing ongoing behavior

Although ongoing behavior from students is virtually inevitable, your efforts should focus on preventing it. You already have learned many techniques to prepare students for Corrective Teaching. The relationships you develop with your students are strengthened by your consistent use of these various teaching methods and make it more likely that students will accept your feedback.

Preventive Teaching – A student is more likely to meet your expectations if you explain them before you do Corrective Teaching. One of the first things you should preventively teach all students is how to accept criticism and consequences. All students will receive

considerable feedback each day to help them develop a better repertoire of behaviors. Teaching them how to accept criticism contributes to their future success.

Students who have difficulties accepting criticism will need frequent prompting prior to your feedback so that they are able to internalize that skill.

As students begin to consistently use the skill of "Accepting Criticism," you should begin to move from simply requiring student compliance toward teaching self-management strategies. Teaching a range of skills (disagreeing or interrupting appropriately, anger control, giving negative feedback, expressing feelings appropriately, conflict resolution, self-monitoring, and reflection) will help students "read" social situations, review their options, and choose the best response (Dowd & Tierney, 1992).

Praise – Using various forms of praise helps maintain or increase desirable behaviors and build relationships with your students. Praise is your most powerful tool for changing behavior. Students who are frequently reinforced for positive behavior are less likely to act out to get your attention. If a student has a large "reinforcement reserve" (i.e., tangibles, privileges, or social reinforcers from others or himself or herself), the student is less likely to react inappropriately to a consequence or criticism. It is your responsibility to help the student develop a reinforcement reserve by noticing his or her positive behaviors and rewarding them.

Corrective Teaching – The Teaching Interaction is used when minor misbehaviors occur. Intervening early, when behaviors are "small," will help students learn your expectations and tolerances, possibly preventing escalation of inappropriate behavior.

▶ The process

Ongoing behavior can occur at any time during the Teaching Interaction, but it happens most often during these certain steps: "Description of the Inappropriate Behavior," "Consequence," "Request for Acknowledgment," and "Practice." During each of these steps, students are either receiving corrective feedback or being asked to participate in the Teaching Interaction. By knowing where ongoing behavior is most likely to occur, you can use preventive measures like prompts and praise to reduce the chances of it happening.

The following sections explain the various methods that can be used when you first respond to a student's ongoing behavior.

Helping the student regain self-control

When ongoing behavior occurs, stop the Teaching Interaction and deal with the inappropriate behaviors. The following methods are designed to help shape behavior and promote student self-control.

1. Coupling statements – These are brief descriptions of inappropriate behavior paired with descriptions of a more appropriate alternative. Example: "You're slouched in your chair. Please sit up."

Observe what the student is doing and describe the most overt or intrusive behavior. For example, if a student is arguing in a loud voice tone, waving his arms, and glaring at you, the behavior you should address is the arguing. Loud arguing is probably the most disruptive behavior, and you would have difficulty doing any further teaching until it diminishes or stops. You might say, "Instead of arguing, please be quiet."

Avoid vague or judgmental terms by keeping your descriptions specific. Use brief statements and matched behavioral pairs that include a description of both the inappropriate behavior and the appropriate alternative behavior. Avoid describing the absence of a behavior, since it doesn't give the student an alternative behavior that could replace what he or she is doing.

Example:

(Specific)

"You're tapping your pencil on the table. Please set it down."

(Nonspecific)

"That's really obnoxious. Would you stop that?"

Example:

(Brief)
"You're standing. Please sit down."

(Lengthy)
"You're standing up with your hands on your hips, shaking your head from side to side, and moving your mouth without saying anything. Please sit down, put your hands in your lap, and keep your head and mouth still."

Example:

(Matched pairs)
"You're pacing. Please stand still."

(Unmatched pairs)
"You're pacing. Please stop pacing" or *"You're pacing. Please be quiet."*

If you vary your word choice, you'll avoid badgering the student, which usually escalates negative behavior. Avoid overusing any one particular phrase, especially those that may set off a power struggle, such as "You need to..." or "I want you to...."

Although giving simple instructions is acceptable (e.g., "Please sit down"), coupling statements provide clear behavioral contrasts and make students more aware of what they're doing. Perhaps the most important function of a "coupling statement" is that it serves as a check on your emotions. That is, if you are focused primarily on observing and describing the student's behavior, you are less likely to react emotionally, thereby worsening the situation.

2. Specific praise – Provide the student with specific praise to reinforce any appropriate behavior you want to maintain. Praise the student for any instructions he or she follows. For example, if you ask a student, "Instead of turning away from me, would you please face me?", and he follows that instruction, you should tell him, "Thanks for turning and looking at me."

Recognizing any effort the student makes and reinforcing behavioral approximations helps the student regain self-control and maintain desired behaviors. For example, if

you ask a student who is yelling to be quiet, you should praise her when she lowers her voice (e.g., "Nice job of lowering your voice.").

By praising any of the student's prosocial behaviors, you increase the likelihood that the behavior will continue or be used more frequently. Reinforcing the student's progress in regaining self-control is a key to this shaping process.

3. Rationales or "reality" statements – Rationales help students understand the benefits of following your instructions. Pointing out the positive outcomes of regaining self-control helps students make better choices about their behavior.

Example: *"If you can calm down and be quiet, we'll be able to take care of this more quickly."*

Knowing what reinforces a student and including it in your rationale also can help motivate change.

Example: *"When you look at me and answer calmly, we are more likely to finish this discussion in time for you to have lunch with your friends."*

"Reality" statements can help explain to students what you expect from them in a given situation. Many students have found through previous experience that certain behaviors, though inappropriate, get them what they want, which sometimes is to be left alone. By persisting in those behaviors, students find they can frustrate adults and achieve that goal. Adults may abandon their efforts and unintentionally reinforce the maladaptive behaviors. "Reality" statements (e.g., "We're sure not getting much accomplished this way" or "Are you really getting what you want here?") let students know you won't go away and that you will help them resolve the issue, thus breaking the cycle of reinforcement.

4. Empathy statements – A statement that lets the student know that you understand his or her situation or experiences can help de-escalate a problem behavior. Such a statement might start out like, "I know it's difficult to accept someone's criticism...." Often, simply recognizing that a student is experiencing something difficult can help alleviate some of the ongoing behavior.

5. Positive correction statements – If you issued the student a negative consequence during your Teaching Interaction, a positive correction statement may also give the student incentive to make better behavioral choices. You may want to let the student know what can be earned back by following your instructions. Simple contingency management often serves to increase desired behaviors. An example of a positive correction statement would be, "When you start following instructions, you'll begin earning back some of the recess time you lost."

Now let's put all of these steps together in an example classroom situation:

Heather is a seventh-grader who has been off task for several minutes. You asked her to get back to work, but she remained off task. You approach her and initiate a Teaching Interaction on staying on-task.

Start a Teaching Interaction

"Heather, I know this assignment may be somewhat difficult for you, but just a moment ago, you were looking around the room, tapping your pencil on your desk, and yawning. "

Heather begins to argue about her behavior.

Stop the Teaching Interaction

Attempt to help the student regain control through "coupling" statements, specific praise, rationales, "reality" statements, and empathy.

Coupling statements

"Heather, you're talking loudly. Please be quiet and listen right now." (Pause)

Praise and coupling statements

"I appreciate your looking at me and staying seated, but you're still talking loudly; please be quiet." (Pause)

Rationale

"You know, Heather, when you're quiet, we can get this taken care of a lot quicker and you can finish your essay a lot sooner." (Pause)

Empathy and coupling statements

"I know you have some concerns about your assignment, but we can't discuss them when you're yelling. Please be quiet." (Pause)

Praise

"Nice job lowering your voice, Heather. That way I know you're getting ready to calmly talk about this with me." (Pause)

"I appreciate you looking at me, and you're quiet now, too. Thanks, Heather." (Pause)

Acknowledgment

"Looks like we can finish this now, okay?"

(Heather acknowledges.)

How you use the components of this technique will depend on how a student responds. Always be aware of your own behavior – use a calm, modulated voice tone; avoid harsh, demanding instructions; pause often to allow the student to respond. You may even need to talk while the student is talking, but be careful not to "talk over" the student. If the student raises his or her voice, lower yours; the student may be influenced by your modeling, or may lower his or her voice to be able to hear you.

Avoid responding directly to demands or accusations (i.e., "getting into content") to prevent a power struggle between you and the student. Address the student's arguing by using the techniques discussed earlier in this section. Although a student may have a valid issue to discuss, addressing it now may reinforce an inappropriate way to bring up concerns with people. Consider this example: A student says, "You're so unfair! How come you like everyone else better than me?" You respond with, "I can see you have some issues you'd like to discuss with me and I'd be happy to set a time later today for us to

talk (empathy). But instead of trying to talk about it now, you need to just be quiet and listen (coupling statement) so that we can finish this and move on with class (rationale)."

Continue this shaping process as long as the student demonstrates improvement. The more praise you provide for behavioral approximations, the more likely you are to see positive change. However, if the negative behaviors are escalating and you see no improvement, or the student is replacing one inappropriate behavior with another, you can begin the office referral process that will be explained later in this chapter. Your goal is to keep the student in the classroom, if possible, so he or she doesn't lose instruction time.

Completing the Teaching Interaction(s)

Once you have helped the student regain self-control and have reinforced all behavioral progress with specific praise, move on to completing your teaching. Since your goal is to teach the student the skills that best meet his or her needs, assess each situation and each student individually and teach accordingly.

There are three basic ways to continue and complete your teaching once a student has regained self-control. You may choose to: 1) teach in response to the ongoing behavior and the behavior that led to the original Teaching Interaction; 2) teach in response to only the ongoing behavior; or 3) return to the original Teaching Interaction. Whatever choice you make, you must complete a Teaching Interaction that includes consequences for the behaviors you address.

If you decide to **teach in response to the original behavior and the ongoing behavior (Example 1)**, you will complete two Teaching Interactions. This decision should be based on the student's need to learn both skills and his or her ability to process this amount of information. One interaction will focus on the original skill deficit. To determine the other skill, you need to consider these factors:

1. Always note the antecedents to the ongoing behavior. For example, if the interfering behavior occurred during the "Consequence" step, you may want to teach the student how to accept a consequence or how to disagree appropriately. If the student has difficulty when you ask him or her to practice, you may teach him how to follow instructions. Teaching how to accept criticism would be the logical choice if a student engages in negative behaviors during the "Description of the Inappropriate Behavior" step.

2. It's also critical to consider the student's individual needs. Ask yourself questions like, "What skill does this student frequently have trouble with?"; "What skill will provide the greatest assistance in different situations?"; and "What can I teach that will allow this student to better manage his or her own behavior?" These questions will help guide your decisions, particularly with students who have progressed from needing compliance-based skills toward self-management skills.

3. Frequently, your second Teaching Interaction will be about accepting criticism or a consequence. Most ongoing behavior comes from students who are in the acquisition stage of social skills learning. In order for these students to progress to higher-level skills, they need to increase their fluency with the critical skills of "Accepting Criticism or a Consequence," and "Following Instructions."

Once you've decided to teach two skills and have determined which skills to teach, move into the Ongoing Behavior Teaching Interaction. Tell the student that you will return to the original behavior, but first you need to discuss the ongoing behavior.

Proceed with your teaching in response to the ongoing behavior just as you would with any Teaching Interaction. (For the sake of continuity, we will continue with the example involving Heather, the seventh-grader.)

Example 1

Start the Ongoing Behavior Teaching Interaction

"Before we can talk about staying on task, Heather, we first need to discuss how you just accepted that criticism. **(Transition Statement)** *When I tried to talk to you about being off-task, you argued with me."* **(Description of Inappropriate Behavior)**

"Remember, whenever someone gives you criticism, you need to look at them, say 'Okay,' and not argue." **(Description of Appropriate Behavior)**

"When you can accept criticism without arguing, you won't make the situation worse." **(Rationale)**

"Does that make sense? Tell me how you're going to accept criticism." **(Request Acknowledgment)**

Heather gives skill steps.

Now return to the original Teaching Interaction and include a Preventive Prompt to increase the student's chances for success at accepting the rest of your criticism/consequences.

"And you'll get another chance to practice accepting criticism because we need to finish talking about you being off-task. Remember to look at me and not argue, okay?" **(Prompt)**

Complete the original Teaching Interaction sequentially.

Original Teaching Interaction

"Let's talk about staying on-task. Listen carefully to the instructions, begin working carefully, and remain focused on your work." **(Description of Appropriate Behavior)**

"That way you will probably finish your essay and not have to take it home with you." **(Rationale)**

"Let's practice staying on-task. I'm going to go over to check Tyrell's work. While I'm gone, begin working and remain focused on finishing your essay." **(Practice)**

Heather stays on-task and finishes her work.

"All right, Heather! Nice job staying on-task. You worked quietly on your essay and finished another paragraph. Way to go!" **(Feedback)**

"Because you initially had some problems staying on-task and accepting criticism, you weren't able to finish your essay in class. You'll have to take it home and finish it. But, since you practiced both those skills so well, your essay won't be counted as late." **(Consequences)**

"Thanks for working so well with me. Since there are a couple of minutes left in class, why don't you see if you can get another paragraph done before the bell rings." **(General Praise/Redirection)**

Sometimes you may decide that the ongoing behavior represents a greater skill deficit and requires more attention than the original inappropriate behavior. In these situations, you may choose to **teach only to the ongoing behavior (Example 2)**. Previous experiences with the student, in addition to the current one, may indicate that the original issue served only as an antecedent to the "real" problem – accepting your feedback about any type of mistake. You can address the original issue at another time through a delayed practice or by using Effective Praise when the student demonstrates appropriate skill use. In Heather's example, you may notice her staying on-task at another time and reinforce her use of the skill then.

Example 2

Ongoing Behavior Teaching Interaction

"Instead of talking about staying on-task, it looks like we need to discuss how you accepted that criticism." **(Transition Statement)**

"Just now, when I tried to talk to you about being off-task, you argued with me about it." **(Description of Inappropriate Behavior)**

"Remember that whenever you get criticism, you should just look at the person, say 'Okay,' and not argue. Just like you're doing right now." **(Description of Appropriate Behavior)**

"Nice job, Heather. You accepted my criticism without arguing! When you can do that you have a lot more time to spend on your work. Does that make sense?" **(Rationale and Request for Acknowledgment)**

Heather acknowledges.

"Super. Since you had difficulty accepting criticism the first time about being off-task, we had to spend some time talking about the skill. So, you lost quite a bit of work time and you'll probably have to finish your assignment at home. But Heather, since you did such a nice job practicing accepting criticism, I won't count that assignment as late." **(Consequences)**

"Now, why don't you get back to your essay. It's possible you may be able to finish it before the end of class. If you need my help on anything, just raise your hand." **(General Praise/Redirection)**

Teaching in response only to the original behavior (Example 3) will probably occur when the ongoing behavior is fairly brief and of low intensity. If you can help the student regain self-control with a few prompts, cues, and/or coupling statements, simply return to and complete the original Teaching Interaction. It's a good idea to pick up where you left off, unless that involves describing what the student did inappropriately. If you "rehash" the inappropriate behavior, you may risk inciting additional

ongoing behavior. When ongoing behavior occurs at the "Consequences" step, include a preventive prompt before you return to the original Teaching Interaction. This will prepare the student to accept the consequences appropriately.

Example 3

Start a Teaching Interaction

"...but just a moment ago you were looking around the room, tapping your pencil, and yawning." **(Description of Inappropriate Behavior)**

Heather begins to argue.

"Heather, you're talking; please be quiet." **(Coupling Statement/Pause)** *"Great. You're quiet."* **(Praise)**

"Can you keep looking at me too, please?" **(Prompt)** *"Thanks, Heather for looking at me."* **(Praise)** *"I know this assignment may be difficult, but the sooner we finish discussing this, the sooner you can finish the assignment and be done with it."* **(Empathy and Rationale)**

"Instead of looking down at your feet, look up at me. That way I know you're listening." **(Coupling Statement/Rationale)** *"Nice job looking at me and following that instruction. Let's continue, okay? Remember to just look at me and say 'Okay.'"* **(Praise/Preventive Prompt)**

Continue with the Original Teaching Interaction

"Nice job, Heather. Whenever you're given a task, get all the materials you need, work

quietly, focus on the task until it's complete, and then let me know when you're finished." **(Description of Appropriate Behavior)**

"If you can do that, you'll probably finish the work a lot quicker and move on to something you enjoy, like reading your novel. Does that make sense? Tell me how to stay on-task." **(Rationale)**

Heather acknowledges and lists steps.

"Okay, let's practice. I'm going to go and help Tyrell. While I'm over there, you'll need to practice staying on-task by finishing the paragraph you're working on right now. Okay? I'll be back in a while to see how you did." **(Practice)**

Heather practices.

"Great job staying on-task! You stayed on-task and got that paragraph finished." **(Feedback)**

"Since you had trouble staying on-task, and we had to discuss and practice it, you didn't have as much time to read your novel. But because you did practice staying on-task so nicely, you don't have as much of your assignment left to do." **(Consequences)**

"Nice job. Now let's get ready to go to lunch." **(General Praise/Redirection)**

Teach the skill(s) that will be most beneficial to the student and structure your teaching to fit each individual situation. You may need to rearrange some steps to make your teaching more effective. Also, the size of the consequence is determined by the frequency and severity of the behavior. Please refer to Chapter 11, "The Teaching Interaction" for specific discussion of these concepts.

View each student individually. Teach according to each one's needs and the behavioral outcome you are trying to achieve. Don't be too rule-governed or try to follow an exact procedure with every student and situation. Behavior is not an isolated or static event; exchanges occur in a dynamic context, with each aspect related to those that precede or follow it. By recognizing behavior as an interactional, developmental process, you can modify and customize your teaching to meet the needs of all students.

▶ Ongoing Behavior Teaching Interaction into Administrative Intervention

In the first part of this chapter, you learned how to prevent or de-escalate ongoing behaviors that interfere with the learning process. When these methods are effective, students regain self-control so you can complete your teaching and they can remain in your classroom. However, there will be situations when students won't respond to your efforts. When this happens, they need to leave the classroom to receive additional, individualized attention from an administrator. (See Chapter 14, "Overview of Administrative Intervention.")

In this section, we will discuss the process of referring a disruptive student to the office. Keep in mind that **you** decide when to begin the referral process. Your decision should be based on the severity and duration of the behaviors and whether the student is showing progress toward the goal of regaining self-control.

Definition

The referral process is not a separate type of Teaching Interaction. It is not a fixed series of steps that is to be used at a designated point in time, or following a particular set of behaviors. Rather, it is a flexible teaching sequence designed to help the student recognize the severity and consequences of his or her behavior, and to provide behavioral alternatives. It includes many of the same techniques discussed earlier in this chapter, but also employs the use of consequences. The sequence is flexible because you can easily return to the original teaching agenda if a student regains self-control. The sequence is fair because you continue to communicate expectations and outcomes to a student throughout the process.

Purpose and timing

The main purpose of the referral sequence is to help the student regain self-control while you continue your teaching focus. Using clear instructions, praise, and rationales helps students understand their options and make better decisions about their behavior.

The most logical time to utilize the referral sequence is when a student displays ongoing behavior that continues or escalates during a Teaching Interaction. If, at any time, a student's behavior is perceived as dangerous to the student or others, all steps should be bypassed and the student should immediately be referred to the office. Examples of behavior that would result in an immediate referral include, but are not limited to, verbal or physical abuse or assault, major destruction of property, and being under the influence of drugs or alcohol. Your school or school district probably has a list of major offenses that result in removal of a student from a classroom. Additional discussion of types of office referral behavior is found in Chapter 14, "Overview of Administrative Intervention."

The process

Whenever you begin to discuss students' behavior with them, it is hoped that they will accept feedback and consequences without arguing, complaining, or demonstrating any other interfering behaviors. Unfortunately, this doesn't always happen. When disruptive behaviors do arise, you must deal with the ongoing behavior in order to teach needed skills. Little learning can take place if the student continues engaging in negative behaviors while you are trying to teach. Your main goal is to help the student regain control so he or she can remain in the classroom. As such, the first task is to help the student identify inappropriate behaviors and replace them with more appropriate ones. The following section explains each step in the office referral process. Examples are used to illustrate the steps.

Help the student regain self-control. Once you've recognized the student's ongoing behavior, you should provide clear descriptions of the negative behavior and alternative appropriate behaviors to help the youth make better decisions. As described earlier in this chapter, these paired statements should focus on correcting one behavior at a time. Describing too many behaviors can confuse the student and have a "badgering" effect that can escalate negative behavior. Descriptions should emphasize the behaviors that are the most overt and disruptive to your teaching at that moment. Examples include: "You're arguing. It would be better if you'd be quiet and listen"; "You have your head on your desk. I'd like you to sit up and look at me, please"; and "You're standing up. Please sit down." Coupling the inappropriate behavior with an alternative behavior lets the student know what should and shouldn't be done.

After each instruction, pause to allow adequate time for the student to respond. The pauses should be long enough to give the student a chance to calm down, but short enough that they don't reinforce inappropriate behavior. Don't expect immediate compliance; it's difficult for most people to follow instructions after they have lost self-control. Praise any approximations of desirable behaviors. These may be the specific behaviors you asked for, or any others you observe. The descriptions should be brief and specific. Let's look at an example of a situation in which the referral process is used.

Example

David is a ninth-grade student. While you're talking with him about forget-ting his social studies homework, he begins to argue.

Student : David is standing by his desk, arguing loudly and pointing his finger.

Teacher: *"David, you're talking loudly. I'd like you to be quiet and listen."* (Pause)

Student: David lowers his voice, crosses his arms, turns his back to you, and continues arguing.

Teacher: *"Thanks for lowering your voice. You're continuing to talk. Please stop talking and listen."* (Pause)

Student: David continues the disruptive behaviors.

Teacher: *"It's great that you're standing still and staying right here, but you're still arguing. We could take care of this a lot quicker if you would be quiet and listen."* (Pause)

Using empathy statements and rationales, as discussed earlier in this chapter, also may help the student regain self-control. Continue using a combination of these techniques as long as the student is making progress. However, if the student's ongoing behavior continues or escalates, you'll need to move on to the next step of the process.

Give a moderate consequence. Letting the student know that he or she has earned a moderate consequence indicates the seriousness of the behavior. A moderate consequence may motivate the student to stop the inappropriate behaviors and begin engaging in more appropriate behaviors. A moderate consequence should be predetermined by the teacher, but may entail the loss of a privilege (recess time, computer use, staying after school, or a note or call home to the parents).

Give specific instructions (paired statements, empathy, or rationales). If the moderate consequence does not stop the student's ongoing behavior (and it sometimes will not), you should again provide some paired statements to help the student move toward more desirable behaviors. As mentioned before, your descriptions should focus on the most overt behaviors. If you have described one particular behavior throughout the process and the student hasn't improved that behavior, you may want to switch your focus to a different inappropriate behavior, as illustrated in the next example.

Your choice of strategies and the length of time you spend on this step will depend on what you know about the student and what you observe. Whereas paired descriptions are very helpful to one student, empathy statements or rationales may work best for another. Some students may be able to regain self-control fairly quickly, while others will demonstrate slow, but steady improvement. In general, though, unless the student is beginning to demonstrate real progress toward regaining self-control, you'll need to start thinking about how the disruption is affecting the other students in your classroom. Giving the student too much attention at this point also may serve to reinforce the student's loss of self-control.

Example

Student: David continues to stand by his desk. He turns around to face you and places his fists on his hips. He sighs loudly and begins to argue.

Teacher: *"Thanks for looking at me, David. You're standing up. Would you sit down, please?"* (Pause)

Tell the student an office referral is possible. If the student does not respond to your instructions, or escalates the inappropriate behavior, state that an office referral is possible if the ongoing behavior continues. This indicates the seriousness of the situation and what will happen if the behavior isn't stopped.

Letting students know about the consequences they will receive if they don't regain self-control helps establish a tie between the behavior and the consequences. The student should realize that he or she determines what happens next – either stop the negative behavior or earn the negative consequences. By understanding this basic concept – that they can control the outcome of a situation by controlling their behavior – students hopefully will choose to avoid the major consequence and the office referral.

Example

Student: David continues his ongoing behaviors.

Teacher: *"If you continue to argue with me and not follow my instructions, you will need to report to the office."* (Pause)

Refer the student to the office. If the student continues to behave inappropriately after you have described the possible negative consequences, he should immediately be referred to the office. Your attempts to help the student regain self-control have not been successful, so in fairness to the student and the others in your classroom, an office referral is necessary. Once in the office, the student will receive additional one-on-one attention and teaching from an administrator in order to learn better ways of dealing with problems in the classroom and other situations. (See Chapter 14, "Overview of Administrative Intervention.") The combination of teaching and consequences should help the student learn self-control and what to do to avoid an office referral in the future.

When making the actual office referral, tell the student he has earned a major consequence and to report to the office. Ask the student if he can get there on his own or if he needs assistance. The student no longer has the option of staying in your classroom, but might not get up and leave on his own. In this situation, you'll need to follow predetermined procedures for getting help. In any case, the final decision on how a student reports to the office is left to the student, giving him another opportunity to make choices about his behavior. Choosing whether to report on his own or with assistance can affect the level of consequences that go with the office referral.

Example

Student: David remains standing and continues to argue.

Teacher: *"David, for arguing and not following instructions, you need to report to the office. Can you get there by yourself, or do you need some help?"*

Once you've made the office referral, the administrator assumes the responsibility of dealing with the student's behavior until the intervention sequence is completed. Inform the office of the referral by the prearranged method (e.g., intercom, telephone, student assistant). At the same time, let the office know whether the student needs assistance.

Example

Student: David says *"Fine!"* in a loud voice and leaves your room, slamming the door on the way out.

Teacher: Calls office via intercom. *"David Rogers has been referred to the office. He's on his way."*

or

Student: David sits down in his chair, crosses his arms, looks away, and says nothing.

Teacher: Calls office via intercom. *"David Rogers has been referred to the office. He needs assistance."*

Hopefully, the student will quietly leave the classroom and report directly to the office. Should he refuse to leave the classroom, your main concern still is with your other students. Trying to teach the student additional skills at this time would be unproductive, at best. Paying attention to his refusal may only serve to reinforce that behavior and give the student an "audience" in front of the other students. As long as he is not disturbing others, the student may remain in your class until an administrator arrives. (Of course, this is assuming that an administrator or crisis interventionist is in the building and will arrive within minutes of the referral.)

What if the student not only refuses to leave the classroom, but also is being disruptive or destructive? In these cases, your best option is to instruct the other students to leave the classroom with you. Moving your class to the hall, media center, or multipurpose room is preferable to attempting physical restraint or allowing the out-of-control student to demonstrate such behavior in front of an audience. Leaving the student alone may help de-escalate the youth's behavior. And, you will ensure that the rest of the class isn't at risk of getting hurt. Consequences, including any necessary compensation, should be given by the administrator during the office referral process.

▶ General considerations

When you are dealing with a student who is engaging in ongoing behavior, monitor your own behavior very carefully. It is very easy to allow yourself to get caught up in the student's words and actions. You may feel angry, agitated, or frustrated when a student is not following your instructions or accepting your feedback. Therefore, you have to be aware of your own behavior. Concentrate on keeping a calm, nonthreatening voice tone and body posture.

Responding with harsh, aggressive behavior, in all likelihood, will only escalate the student's negative behavior.

A calm, quiet voice tone models your expectations and may help the youth to regain self-control. Trying to "talk over" a student results in a cycle of each person speaking louder than the other, eventually leading to a shouting match and accompanying feelings of anger. You may have to pause and take a deep breath in order to avoid the impulse to speak loudly. It also allows the student to hear, understand, and begin to comply with what you've said.

Remember that this is not a time to justify your role, explain fairness, or address the student's complaints or issues. Even though you may feel like responding to what a student is saying, don't get drawn into arguments or discussions. The easiest way to avoid this trap is to respond only to the behavior of **talking**, not to what the youth is saying. The overriding goal is to help the student calm down. Once this is accomplished, you can set a separate time for the student to discuss concerns with staff members.

There are many advantages to not arguing with a student. You'll not only avoid losing your own self-control and possibly escalating the student's behavior, but you'll also maintain your relationship with the student. You won't risk saying something hurtful or negative to the student if you keep your focus on the student's **behavior** of talking or arguing rather than on the words that are being said.

Maintain a safe, appropriate distance between the student and you. Stay at least an arm's length away; you don't want the student to feel "closed in" or physically pressured. If the student feels trapped, he or she may strike out or try to run away. Touching, in most cases, is not recommended when dealing with an agitated student. Any type of touch or certain hand gestures at this time may be perceived as aversive or threatening. Reaching out, pointing at the student, or clenching your fists may send strong, negative messages to the student. A less-threatening posture may be to keep your hands at your sides, in your pockets, or folded in front of you.

Always remember to allow a pause after you've given an instruction to the student. Pausing allows the student to hear, understand, and begin to comply with what you've said. "Rapid-fire" instructions may confuse children and may escalate their negative behaviors. Counting to yourself between instructions may help you maintain an appropriate pace.

▶ Summary

You may find that your most powerful tool in preventing ongoing behavior is consistent teaching and recognition of a student's efforts. Clearly communicating your expectations and following up with praise and Corrective Teaching show your concern and fairness, and help build strong relationships with students. These relationships, in turn, may help students bring their behavior under control in stressful situations. At the very least, even if you are unsuccessful in helping a student remain in your class after he or she has lost self-control, the student's

return to your room will be easier because your relationship with the student has remained intact.

CHAPTER THIRTEEN

Behavior contracting

Sometimes in your efforts to teach students social skills you may find it difficult to motivate them to change their behavior. Behavior contracting with students can be an effective method to promote behavior change as a less restrictive method than a daily token system. In fact, a contract system can be useful when fading a more frequent reward system, or for older students who still need more stringent consistencies but with less restraint.

Behavior contracting is a technique used to structure behavioral intervention by making each of the necessary elements of the process so clear and explicit that they may be written into an agreement for behavior change that is understandable and acceptable to everyone involved (DeRisi & Butz, 1975). Simply stated, a behavior contract is a structured means of exchanging positive reinforcement between two persons for fulfill-

ment of specified responsibilities. The agreement explains the requirement to be met or task to be completed, and the consequence for fulfillment of that requirement. In this chapter, we will discuss the elements of an effective behavior contract.

Behavior contracts are not just used in classrooms; they are a part of our everyday adult life. We sign contracts with employers that specify our job responsibilities and our compensation; we contract with a bank when we make a major purchase, such as buying a home or a car. When contracts are unclear, they are more difficult to abide by or sign. Imagine, for example, signing a teacher contract without knowing what your pay would be, or what the specific job expectations were. Therefore, student contracts must be governed by such behavioral principles as contingency, specificity, shaping, and positive reinforcement.

► # The elements of a behavior contract

An effective behavior contract needs to include several key elements. They are the specification of:

> 1. the task to be completed
>
> 2. the performance criteria
>
> 3. the consequence

Specifying the task to be completed

Before writing the contract, you must specify the task to be completed. In selecting the task, consider several things. Many times students have a multitude of problem behaviors. However, beginning with just one behavior may often affect many other behaviors that you may want to remediate in the future. Consider choosing a behavior that has gone unrewarded or been punished in the past, and one that is functional for the student. That is, if the chosen behavior is performed more frequently, it will increase the student's chances of getting more of the natural kinds of rewards from the people in his or her environment. For example, helping a student speak to teachers in a socially acceptable manner may result in less criticism and increased rewards for appropriate school behavior (DeRisi & Butz, 1975).

The behavior must be specifically described in observable, measurable terms. In order to accomplish this, you may want to ascertain where and when the behavior occurs, who is present at that time, the frequency of the behavior, etc.

The contract also must be achievable for the student. Therefore, determine at what level the student is currently performing the behavior, and set the goal at a level which can be mastered. That way, the student can successfully complete the contract. You may also wish to start with a task that does not require a great deal of time to complete.

Specifying the performance criteria

Once you have selected the target behavior, write the contract jointly with the student. Remember that a contract cannot be imposed upon a student; rather, it must be agreed upon by both parties. Let the student know that the contract is open to renegotiation at any time (Rhode, Jensen, & Reavis, 1992). This allows the student to realize that you are willing to listen to his or her input and demonstrates your concern about the student's perception of how the contract is working.

The contract should be stated in positive terms and indicate to what criteria the task is to be performed (e.g., how well, for what length of time, how often, etc.). For example, Elvis is a seventh-grader who has difficulty completing classroom math assignments. His contract might stipulate that he needs to finish three out of five of those assignments to 80 percent accuracy in order to earn his specified reward: 20 minutes of time playing the computerized music program on Friday afternoon.

According to *The Tough Kid Book* (Rhode et al., 1992), contracts should have performance criteria that specify either consecutive or cumulative requirements. Contracts that use consecutive performance criteria are the least desirable because they require a student to perform the behavior for a specified consecutive number of days prior to receiving the consequence. That leaves little room for error. On the other hand, a contract with cumulative performance criteria is optimal. It allows students to be successful because they can recover from their mistakes and still meet their goals. In the previous example, Elvis is much more likely to be successful if he is required to complete assignments for any three out of the five school days instead of three days in a row.

Specifying the consequence

Finally, negotiate with the student regarding the consequence that can be earned. Students are much more likely to work for a reward they have the privilege of choosing. Involving children in the selection of their rewards communicates that their efforts at changing their behavior are appreciated. Many times, using children's suggestions results in establishing more fair, accurate, and rewarding contingencies, which in turn, increases the likelihood that behavior change will occur and be maintained over time (Kelley, 1990).

In discussing with Elvis what would motivate him to complete his math assignments, his teacher learned that he found music to be the most reinforcing. Elvis then indicated that being able to practice his songwriting skills would motivate him to complete his math. As it worked out, the behavior and consequence were closely related. His math class was working on fractions and songwriting requires the use of fractions in the development of time signatures. Of course, if this consequence is to be truly rewarding to Elvis, it must be absolutely contingent on the behavior of completing his homework. That is, he should not have access to the privilege of working on his songwriting at any other time during the day.

Consequences must be easily attainable and neither expensive nor time-consuming. Sometimes, parents wish to deliver the contingent reinforcement in the home. If you use this consequence method, you must communicate routinely with parents, either through progress notes or school notes. Regardless of where the reinforcer is delivered, the contract should have some type of tracking system to indicate what levels of achievement have been reached. A simple grid at the bottom of the contract can easily record that information.

Some contracts may include a penalty clause for not meeting the contingency, or a bonus clause for exceeding the expected criteria (Rhode et al., 1992). The use of penalty clauses should be limited to contracts that have been utilized and proven to be reinforcing to the student in the past, and/or the performance criteria has been established as accurate. An example of a penalty clause that could be included in Elvis's contract might be that if he doesn't complete his math classwork to the specified criteria, he has to finish it during free time on Friday. A bonus for Elvis, such as extra time on the computerized music program, could be given for achieving higher than 85 percent on assignments, or completing more than three days' assignments. After the contingencies are agreed upon, you and the student sign the contract.

Monitoring & evaluating the contract

Each day, the teacher and/or the student monitor and evaluate the student's progress on the contract. At the end of the contract, either the consequence is delivered, the contract is revised, or both. If a student fulfills the contract, a new one may be written for the same performance criteria or be changed to include more stringent criteria. In any case, the contract must be evaluated based on the student's performance. If a bonus was easily obtained, the criteria should be modified accordingly. The same is true if the student did not achieve criteria.

If the contract is unsuccessful

If the student does not meet the criteria established in the contract, the contract may need modifications. Prior to changing the contract, there are several things to look at to improve the contract. First, make sure the student understood the contract process. If the student is confused, the behavior may not have been defined or explained clearly enough. The Preventive Teaching process is helpful in clarifying expectations for the student. (See Chapter 10.)

It also is important to evaluate whether the task requirement was reasonable and specific. If the student understands the process but has difficulty meeting the task requirement, the teacher may need to add smaller steps to help the student complete the task. For example, the contract currently states that Elvis is expected to complete all of his math work. If that expectation is too difficult for Elvis to achieve at this time, his teacher may need to alter the criteria in order for him to achieve success. He may instead be required to complete 8 out of the 10 problems.

You also may need to examine the time frame included in the contract. Elvis may need more frequent reinforcement than every Friday. If this is the case, the contract could be rewritten to reward Elvis two out of every three days. Remember, behavior contracts are not as useful for students who continually need higher rates of reinforcement, (e.g., students who need a token system or very young children).

Always ensure that the task requirement is not judged arbitrarily and that the student clearly understands what is required. There should be no subjectivity in determining whether or not criteria is achieved; rather, achievement of the specified goal should be clearly measurable.

The success criterion also must be evaluated. The contract's goal should be attainable for the student. If it is not, the contract will be ineffective and the student will not progress. The concept of shaping should always be used when setting goals in behavior contracts. For example, a problem with Elvis's contract may be that he currently gets 65 percent on his math work; therefore, 80 percent may be too high for him to attain at the onset. Also, specify an amount of time in which the contract is to be fulfilled. That is, utilize cumulative performance criteria versus consecutive.

Finally, the reinforcing value of the consequence needs to be evaluated. This pitfall is easily avoided if the student is involved in creating the behavior contract. The size of the consequence should correspond with the size of the behavior. If Elvis receives only five minutes of computer time for three hours of math work, that consequence will probably not be reinforcing enough to motivate him to fulfill the contract.

▶ Summary

Behavior contracts can help teachers build good working relationships with seemingly unmotivated students. If contracts are clearly written, positively stated, and include student input, you can achieve success in helping students change their behavior in relatively short periods of time. The key is to start at the student's current performance level and shape to the desired goal, one step at a time.

Sample behavior contracts are included on the following pages.

CONTRACT

TASK

Who: _____Theresa C._____

What: _____turn homework in on time_____

When: _____3rd period English_____

How Well: _____2 times per week_____

_____(2 out of 5 days)_____

_____

CONSEQUENCE

Who: _____Theresa C._____

What: _____homework free Friday_____

When: _____for each 2 to 5 days_____

How Much: _____1 Friday_____

_____

_____

Sign Here: _____Theresa C._____ Date: __11/4__

Sign Here: _____Mrs. Criste_____ Date: __11/4__

TASK RECORD

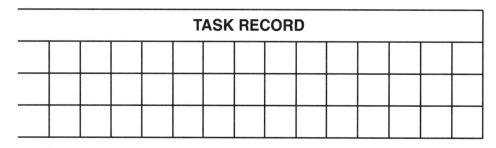

CONTRACT

TASK	CONSEQUENCE

TASK

Who: _Bob W._

What: _ignore other students' behavior in class_

When: _Mon - Fri. - 3rd period_

How Well: _Four days (not in a row)_
without "tattling" to the teacher about
peer behavior

CONSEQUENCE

Who: _Bob W._

What: _special teacher helper to Mrs. Smith_

When: _on day 5_

How Much: _1 school day_

Sign Here: _Mrs. Smith_   Date: _10/1_

Sign Here: _Bob W._   Date: _10/1_

TASK RECORD

10/2	10/3	10/4	10/5	10/8	10/9	10/10								
	wow!	—	!	—	—	YES								
MS	MS		MS			MS								

CONTRACT

(I/We), _____ *Elvis* _____, hereby declare
(who)

that (I, we) will _____ *complete in-class math assignment* _____
(does what)

_____

This job will be considered successful _____ *when 3 of 5 days* _____

assignments are completed and at 80% accuracy.
(how well)

_____ *Elvis* _____
(signed)

For the successful completion of the above job you may

_____ *receive 20 minutes of computer time with the music program.* _____

Date Signed _____ *9/26* _____

Date Completed _____

_____ *C. Nelson* _____
(signed)

CHAPTER FOURTEEN

Overview of administrative intervention

So far, you have learned techniques for dealing with ongoing behavior or loss of self-control. However, as described in Chapter 12, you can face situations when a student can no longer stay in the classroom because of the frequency, intensity, or severity of the ongoing behavior. In these situations, the student is referred to the school office, where the principal or another staff member intervenes to help the student regain self-control. We call this process Administrative Intervention.

This chapter provides guidelines for determining when to refer a student to the office, an overview of Administrative Intervention, and an explanation of your role in the referral process.

▶ When to refer a student

The office referral process gives teachers a series of steps to follow when a student is unable to bring his or her behavior under control. This process, which was described in Chapter 12, should cover as many as 90 percent of the situations in which office referrals are necessary.

There are three main patterns of student behavior that can lead to an office referral. Two of the three are preceded by teaching; the third type results in an automatic referral.

Automatic referrals occur whenever a student commits a **major infraction of a school rule** or engages in a **serious misbehavior**, particularly one that endangers the safety of that student or others.

This type of referral should be fairly infrequent because it represents behaviors of considerable magnitude. Depending on what the student does, little or no teaching may precede the referral. Examples include fighting; possession of weapons, drugs, gang-related paraphernalia, or other contraband; major destruction of property; being under the influence of drugs or alcohol; and physical or verbal aggression that is perceived as threatening. Such aggression would include striking out at you or another student, or getting physically close to someone and directly swearing at or threatening that person. You may need to use some of the techniques for calming a student who is displaying ongoing behavior, but most of these situations also require help from others.

Again, the frequency of automatic referrals should be fairly low. If you find you are referring students quite often because of rule infractions, you may want to spend some time evaluating your school policies to see if they are too restrictive. Certainly, major misbehaviors warrant automatic office referrals to ensure the safety and well-being of all students and staff. However, the majority of students' inappropriate behaviors should be dealt with in the classroom. An example may help illustrate this point. In some schools, any swearing by a student results in an automatic office referral. The swearing may or may not be directed at any one person. As a result, some students, given their backgrounds and other difficulties, could find themselves in the office fairly frequently. But unless the behavior (swearing) is so serious that it disrupts or endangers others in the classroom, it may be much more beneficial to use direct skill-based teaching and consequences. By keeping the student in the classroom, you have an opportunity to teach alternative behaviors and the student does not miss valuable instruction time.

The second pattern of behavior that can result in an office referral is the most common of the three types. In this case, the student is engaging in **ongoing behavior** and has been asked several times during one Teaching Interaction to begin following instructions to bring his or her behavior under control. Students most frequently are referred for ongoing behavior related to not following instructions, or not accepting criticism or consequences. Although the ongoing behavior could vary significantly in intensity, duration, and variety, it is not perceived as a threat to the safety of the student or others. Therefore, the teacher has the opportunity to teach alternative behaviors before referring the student to the office for additional help. Chapter 12, "Ongoing Behavior," includes techniques for helping a student regain self-control.

The third pattern of behavior that results in an office referral is **minor misbehavior over time**. These frequent problem behaviors, which require repeated teaching, may occur many times during a single day or class period, or may continue over many days. When using the office as a "back-up" or increased consequence for repeated minor misbehaviors, remember these points:

1. The skill level of the individual student will, in part, determine your use of this office referral option. You may choose to refer a student whom you know has appropriate skills but lately has demonstrated

repeated minor difficulties, such as not having proper school materials or frequently giving criticism to others. On the other hand, a newer or less-skilled student may not be referred for these same behaviors. These students most likely have many other target behaviors that need improvement, and these would take precedence over some of the higher-level "fine tuning" skills. In other words, you should choose consequences and strategies that are in the best interests of each student, based upon his or her skill levels and needs. Otherwise, you may find yourself making too many referrals or falling back on your largest consequences for a variety of misbehaviors.

2. Students should be told that an office referral is probable for continued difficulties. If the behavior continues over time, even with repeated teaching and consequences, you need to let the student know that the situation is becoming serious and that the next step will be an office referral unless some behavioral changes are made. For example, you have talked with a student for the fourth time during one class period about making inappropriate comments. Since the misbehavior is continuing, you feel that the teaching and consequences you've used have been ineffective. At this point, you may tell the student something like, "I need to let you know that if you make any more inappropriate comments to other students during this class period, you'll be referred to the office." This lets the student know what you expect of him or her and what will happen if misbehavior continues.

3. In general, this type of office referral is reserved for one behavior that occurs over time. Sometimes, however, you may tell a student that he or she will be referred to the office for engaging in any of a variety of inappropriate behaviors. This usually occurs when a student begins engaging in a inappropriate behavior as soon as you've finished a Teaching Interaction on a different skill. If this pattern occurs, you may need to increase the in-class consequences or tell the student that any other inappropriate behaviors will result in an office referral. Also, you should check your own behavior by assessing your tolerances for ongoing behavior. It may be that while you're teaching the student, he is doing things that indicate he is not accepting your feedback. Unchecked, these behaviors may escalate or result in "limit-testing" by the student. That is, a student may continue to engage in minor inappropriate behaviors to see how far he can go before you respond.

▶ The Administrative Intervention process

The Administrative Intervention process involves joint efforts and cooperation between the teacher and administrator. The main goal of the process is to help the student regain self-control and to teach alternative behaviors to replace those that resulted in the child's removal from the classroom. Although the immediate teaching agenda focuses on what happened in the classroom, the long-range goal is to teach skills that the student can use to control his or her behavior under any conditions, thereby avoiding negative outcomes such as office referrals, fights, or damaged relationships.

In addition to skill-based teaching, the process allows administrators and teachers to concentrate on building trusting, caring relationships with students. The teaching focus helps students understand that teachers and administrators are genuinely concerned about them, and that the students' behavior, not the students themselves, are at issue.

Step one: Helping the student obtain self-control

After a teacher makes an office referral, the student chooses to report in one of two ways: "in crisis" or "under partial compliance." Preferably, a student will choose to leave the classroom quietly and immediately. If the student goes to the office, is relatively quiet, and follows instructions, but still displays some negative behaviors, he or she is considered "under partial compliance." However, if the student chooses to remain in the classroom following the referral, does not report directly to the office, or reports to the office but is unable to sit quietly, he or she is "in crisis."

The administrator who is working with the student will use a variety of techniques to help the student regain self-control. The goal of this part of the process is to have the youth sit quietly in an assigned place where the student and the administrator can talk. The student also promises to stay in his or her seat while the administrator goes to visit the teacher who made the office referral. The techniques used in the office are similar to those used when dealing with ongoing behavior:

1. Praise – Specific descriptions of a student's progress toward regaining self-control can help the student calm down. Praise is the first thing a student should hear from the administrator upon reporting to the office following a referral. For example, the administrator may say, "Thanks for coming to the office right away." Praise also is used when a student follows specific instructions or approximates desirable behavior.

2. Coupling statements – Using paired descriptions of behavior emphasizes appropriate alternatives to the student's current behavior. An example is, "You're talking. Please be quiet and listen."

3. Simple instructions – Giving simple instructions gives the student options for appropriate behaviors. Examples include, "Please sit down," and "Lower your voice, please."

4. Empathy – Students in crisis often need to know that someone understands their feelings and struggles. By using empathy statements such as "I know this is difficult," or "I understand that you're upset," the administrator can help de-escalate the student's behavior. Empathy statements are often paired with rationales.

5. Rationales – "Process-oriented" rationales are most frequently used during a crisis situation. Statements such as, "The sooner you can quiet down and listen, the sooner we can resolve your issues," let students know that regaining self-control can result in positive outcomes for them.

6. Physical monitoring – While talking with the student, the administrator should be relaxed and move slowly, keeping a safe and comfortable distance from the student to avoid escalating the negative behavior. The goal is to help the student regain control to the point that he or she is able to sit quietly.

Generally, administrators should not block the student's path or restrain the student in any way since physical restraint and management most often escalate behavior. If a student chooses to leave the office area, the administrator should move aside, then follow the student within the school building. In situations where the student might be in danger by leaving the building, an administrator may need to follow or physically keep the student inside. Some schools are near busy streets or highways, and some children may not understand the danger of running out of the building into the street. Administrators should continue to follow set policies about students who leave the school building without permission, but should also be prepared to use physical techniques to keep students safe. Decisions as to the appropriateness of these techniques are left to the trained individual. The National Crisis Prevention Institute in Madison, Wisconsin, is one organization that can provide training and information about physical management.

The administrator works with the student, using a combination of these techniques, until the student is relatively quiet and sitting in the designated spot. At this point, the administrator asks for a verbal commitment from the student that he or she will stay seated in the chair the whole time the administrator is gone. Getting this commitment is necessary for the process to continue, as it represents a "trust bond" between the student and administrator. If the student is not ready to give that commitment, the administrator will not leave. Rather, the administrator will continue working with the student, pointing out continued progress toward the goal, rationales for the process, and potential outcomes of the student's behavior.

The way the administrator asks for the verbal commitment is very important. The wording should specifically ask for the student to stay seated the entire time the administrator is out of the office. By clearly stating this expectation, and having the student agree to it, the administrator can avoid problems that may occur in his or her absence. Consider the potential differences in a student's behavior by changing a few words when gaining a verbal commitment: "I need to know you'll be in this chair when I get back," versus "I need to know that you'll remain seated the entire time I'm gone, and that you'll be here when I get back." Asking the student to stay seated the whole time the administrator is gone does not ensure anything, but it does leave the responsibility and choice of behavior with the student.

If the administrator has any concerns about leaving the student alone in the office because of safety issues, the child would not be left unattended. Rather, another adult would monitor the student during this period of time. Depending on the student's level of compliance, it may be easier to move an adult near the student than to have the student move closer to an available adult.

Step two: Checking with referring teacher

After the student agrees to remain seated, the administrator leaves the office and meets with you (the referring teacher). At that time, the administrator fills out an office referral form (Figure 1) with the information necessary to accurately complete the intervention process. If possible, you should jot some quick notes following the referral so you can provide specific details of your interaction with the student. This information helps the administrator focus on appropriate alternative behaviors to replace those that led to the office referral.

You should be prepared to respond to a number of questions about the referral:

1. Antecedent events – What circumstances surrounded the behavior? Who was involved? Where and when did this occur?

2. Behavioral responses – What did the student do or say? How severe was the behavior? How often does this type of behavior occur? Has it happened frequently in the past?

3. Consequences – How did you intervene? What type of teaching did you attempt? Were any consequences delivered?

4. Additional information – What else can you add to help the administrator work with the student?

The administrator uses this information to determine the type of referral **(serious misbehavior/major rule infraction,** **ongoing behavior, or minor misbehavior over time)** and the skills to teach during the intervention process. The administrator then returns to the office and begins working with the student.

Step three: Intensive Teaching

Upon returning to the office, the administrator should praise the student for staying seated and for anything else the student has done appropriately. If it appears that the student did not stay seated during the administrator's absence (for example, items missing or askew), appropriate consequences for the behavior are given later in the intervention process.

The administrator's goal during Intensive Teaching is to de-escalate the student's disruptive behavior to a point where the student can once again follow instructions. Hopefully, the time the administrator was away has helped the student gain additional self-control. However, if the student continues with partial compliance, the administrator consistently uses the techniques described earlier to help the student achieve this level during the intervention.

During the intervention process, the administrator shapes the student's behavior using coupling statements, specific praise, empathy, and rationales – the same techniques you use when dealing with ongoing behavior and the administrator uses when de-escalating a crisis situation. The administrator works with the student until he or she displays behaviors that indicate a readiness to follow instructions and accept feedback. Acceptable behaviors include being

Figure 1

Office Referral

STUDENT _____ CLASS/TIME _____ REFERRED BY _____

CIRCLE ONE:

MAJOR MISBEHAVIOR/   CONTINUED MINOR MISBEHAVIOR   FAILURE TO ACCEPT
INFRACTION OF SCHOOL RULE   OVER TIME   CRITICISM/CONSEQUENCES

SPECIFIC DESCRIPTION OF PROBLEM BEHAVIOR:

TEACHER INTERVENTION(S):

ADDITIONAL COMMENTS:

quiet, paying attention, and sitting up straight.

Step four: Teaching Interaction

Once the student is displaying appropriate behavior, the administrator starts a Teaching Interaction on the referral behavior. The Teaching Interaction follows the same steps as the one you have learned, but may include extra practices, more discussion, and some problem-solving.

Consequences for the office referral and any other outstanding contracts are given within the context of the Teaching Interaction. If the student's behavior resulted in any other consequences during the office intervention (e.g., damaging the office, prolonged loss of self-control), these also are given at this point. In addition to assigned consequences and potential restitution, each office referral requires notification of parents, an apology to the referring teacher, and completion of all missed classroom assignments.

Throughout the teaching process, the administrator works hard to maintain a sense of fairness and understanding, while helping the student learn better ways to handle difficult situations in the classroom. One goal of the process is to preserve and strengthen the teacher-student relationship; that is, during the intervention, the administrator supports the teacher's decisions while also attending to the student's issues. If an administrator has concerns about the appropriateness of the referral, he or she will talk with the teacher at a separate time.

After all consequences have been delivered, the administrator can allow the student to discuss problems or feelings related to the office referral. At this point, the student has successfully completed the office intervention (except for the apology) and should be able to discuss concerns and feelings rationally. The student and administrator may spend some time problem-solving, working through issues that may have contributed to classroom difficulties, or talking about the student's "side" of the referral. By delaying discussion until this time, the student probably will be more successful in conveying concerns appropriately.

Step five: Prepare and practice apology

The student and the administrator work together on the apology to the referring teacher. The administrator asks questions and helps the student formulate an appropriate apology. A number of practices follow to ensure that the student will be successful when delivering the apology to the teacher. Practices also help the student accept responsibility for his or her own behavior by emphasizing the response chosen by the student. When the administrator feels reasonably confident that the student can successfully make the apology, he or she will return to your classroom to update you on the student's progress and determine if this is a good time for the student to return and give the apology.

Step six: Check with the teacher

When the administrator returns to your classroom, he or she will talk to you about the office intervention and the upcoming apology.

The administrator also will discuss strategies for helping the student return to class successfully. He or she will let you know that the consequences associated with the referral were taken care of, and that no further mention of them is necessary. Reminding the student about negative behavior could result in repeated problems, whereas praise for appropriate behavior will increase the student's chances for successfully returning to class. The administrator may ask about the classwork the student missed while in the office, and encourage the student to talk with you about it.

Step seven: Student delivers apology

After you and the administrator have determined when the student should make the apology, the administrator and student will return to your classroom together. Before returning, however, the administrator probably will have the student practice the apology one more time.

You will be asked to step outside the classroom so the student can apologize away from other students. The administrator will determine whether the apology is acceptable because he or she has been working with the student and has set the expectation level for the student. If the apology does not meet these expectations, the administrator will take the student back to the office for additional teaching and practice. If the apology is acceptable, the administrator will make a statement of approval (e.g., "Nice job, Jan"), or will ask

the student if he or she is ready to return to class. You can then welcome the student back to your class and provide immediate praise for some aspect of the student's behavior.

Following up with frequent praise is also important. By praising the student's efforts, you'll help him or her learn about maintaining relationships even in the face of conflict. Your attention to positive behaviors also communicates that you recognize the attempts the student is making to start anew.

▶ Summary

You have a crucial role in determining the success of the Administrative Intervention process. The following list summarizes your main responsibilities.

1. Consistently maintain low tolerances for inappropriate behaviors and teaching methodologies.

2. Notify appropriate personnel when you have referred a student to the office. Know the proper procedures for notifying the office (e.g., use of intercom, telephone, teacher assistant, or student).

3. Be prepared to clearly describe the antecedent events and student behavior that led to the office referral. Take quick notes following the referral if that will help you be more accurate.

4. Be prepared to provide information about any classwork the student misses. This will ensure that the student is accountable for all assignments.

5. Be ready to accept the student back into your class and to reinforce the apology. You may not always feel ready to have the student back, but the student should be allowed to return following successful completion of the Administrative Intervention process. You can share your specific concerns with the administrator when he or she checks back with you (Step Six), but the administrator makes the final determination about the student's return to the classroom.

6. After the student returns, reinforce any positive behaviors and efforts. The tone and quality of your interactions may well determine how successful the student's reintegration into your classroom is.

CHAPTER FIFTEEN

Working with parents

One of the goals of the Educate America Act states that by the year 2000 every school will promote partnerships that will increase parental involvement and participation in promoting the social, emotional, and academic growth of children (U.S. Department of Education, 1993). The objectives of this goal include, but are not limited to, schools actively engaging families in shared educational decision-making and families holding schools and teachers to high standards of accountability. The school is responsible for building relationships with parents before problems with students arise. This chapter will provide teachers with ways to engender sound working relationships and foster good communication with parents.

The 1991 Council for Exceptional Children Conference in Atlanta established that in the 1990s we can expect to see more of the following: working mothers, latchkey children, cultural and economic diversity, children in poverty, families with special-needs children, homeless families, and children in extended day care. Schools are increasingly charged with the responsibility of providing extended use of their facilities to serve children and their families, particularly those at risk. Often, these parents have had negative relationships with schools when they were students. Thus, they come to their children's schools with preconceived negative expectations. This is exacerbated by the tendency toward bi-directional negative relationships between parents and teachers, particularly when the children are difficult or have special needs. The focus then becomes one of assigning blame rather than finding the best way to help the child. Teachers' low expectations of parents can be an important obstacle to change.

When faced with overwhelming problems, such as those outlined at the CEC Conference, parents are little concerned with engaging in teacher-pleasing behaviors. On the other hand, teachers are pressured to involve parents without adequate resources or time to do so. Few have had the supplemental education to work with parents, nor is it part of their contractual obligations (Betty Phillips Center for Parenthood Education, 1992).

Children spend 6 to 10 hours a day in school and/or extended care programming. Therefore, schools have become responsible for teaching not only academics, but addressing social and emotional issues as well. Without engendering parental support, schools will most likely fail in their efforts to teach children generalizable skills. Parents are their children's first teachers, having taught hundreds of skills before a child enters his first year of school. Obviously, they have the most vested interest in the success or failure of their children. All parents have hopes and goals for their children; they differ in how they support their children's efforts to achieve those goals.

The outcome that teachers glean from developing positive relationships with parents is the ability to provide the best education possible to the students in their charge. In order to achieve that goal, teachers must find methods in which they can develop rapport and build a team relationship with students' families. Parents must also be educated about the school program through teachers' efforts to share information.

Schools tend to take a narrow approach to parent involvement by focusing on one kind of activity, such as parent workshops or a homework hotline (Burch & Palanki, 1994). There must, however, be a varied range of involvement options available to parents that can be tailored to their and their children's individual needs and characteristics. These opportunities should be developmentally appropriate and consistent with the structure, routine, and resources of the school program. Administrators need to ensure that adequate resources are available for work with parents and that teachers are recognized and reinforced for positive interactions with parents (Smallwood, Hawryluk, & Pierson, 1990). Currently, the most common methods used by teachers to communicate with parents are calling on the telephone, holding conferences, and sending notes. These approaches as well as suggested others will be discussed.

▶ Telephone calls

The initial contact with parents sets the stage for all ensuing contact. Being positive and showing interest and enthusiasm, increases the likelihood that parents will engage in reciprocal behavior. It is best to develop open lines of communication before problems arise, preferably at the beginning of the school year. This phone call provides a link and helps parents feel connected to you and the school. It is advisable to ask for the parent's input regarding such things as the child's reinforcers, past experiences, personality, talents, and things to avoid (Kuykendall, 1992). If school is already under way, you may want to spend some time noting the child's strengths. This becomes especially critical when a learning history of negative contacts from teachers has been established for the student in prior grades. Phone calls to parents to share concerns about children's learning or behavior are often unavoidable but they should neither be the first contact made with parents nor the only contact parents have with you. Many parents complain that they only hear about the negative things that their children do. Often, by the time they do receive such a report, the problem is relatively longstanding (Kelley, 1990). The 4:1 positive-to-negative interaction ratio you use with students should hold true for communication with parents as well. Keeping a phone log is an easy way for you to evaluate the frequency and type of calls made. When concern calls are made, there should be a "no fault" emphasis in interactions; the focus should be on how you and the parents can work together to increase the child's success. Any attempts the studnet has made at positive performance should be noted at the beginning of the call and the conversation should end on a positive note.

Sometimes it's difficult for parents and teachers to reach one another because of differing schedules or other logistical issues. Many school programs are trying innovative approaches such as the TransParent School Model (Betty Phillips Center for Parenthood Education, 1992). This model recommends the use of answering machines and voice mail to increase bi-directional contact. It can encompass behavior reports, upcoming school activities, or homework assignments. Parents can call as their schedules permit. The convenience factor has increased contact from parents to the schools who advocate its use.

▶ Conferences

The productive relationships that teachers build with parents provide children with greater consistency in the two most important environments in their lives, thereby increasing opportunities for learning and growth. Stephens and Wolf (1980) recommend a four-step sequence for parent-teacher conferences to maximize the outcome of the meeting.

The first step is building rapport with the parents. Speaking positively about the student conveys a caring attitude. It's best to spend a few moments engaging in small talk to break the ice and to set the stage for a conversation among adult equals.

Second, obtain pertinent information from the parents. Questions such as, "What has Alex told you about?" should open the door for the parents to share information or concerns. Be willing to take some time to discuss the parents' goals for their child throughout the conference.

Third, provide specific information about what the child is doing in school and share samples of his or her work. It is important to share the student's strengths even within an area that requires further development.

Fourth, summarize what was said and discuss any follow-up activities. Parents should also leave the conference with a copy of everything that was discussed.

Your behavior during the conference will greatly determine its outcome. There are several considerations that will enhance the potential for a successful conference. It usually is best to assume that the parents know the most about the child and his or her needs. Always consider the parents' perspective when discussing what you think is best for the child. If making suggestions, start with something that parents can be successful at, and do not be defensive or intimidated if they disagree. Rather, ask for alternatives and be willing to compromise, but also be willing to take a youth advocacy stance on discipline and child protection issues. Most importantly, speak in plain and jargon-free language that is common to both parties to avoid the appearance of being a "teacher expert." If the parents speak another language, an interpreter will be necessary.

▶ Notes

Report cards are sent home too infrequently for parents to have an accurate picture of how their children are faring routinely at school; hence more frequent contact is warranted if the goal is to keep parents informed and to prevent small problems from mushrooming. Written contacts from school can take many forms – from something as simple as a "happy-gram" to more complex newsletters and individualized school notes and progress charts.

Class newsletters that go home regularly are of benefit because they inform parents of everything from curriculum and class activities to upcoming events and even the school lunch menu. In classrooms where a social skill curriculum is being taught, a social skill of the week can be identified and noted

in the newsletter. The steps to the skill can be listed and parents can practice with their child at home in order for the student to generalize the skill. When skills taught at school parallel those taught at home, the overall result is better for the student.

Other methods of keeping parents informed may be through the use of a monthly calendar which notes upcoming events or notes when items are needed for school. It may be helpful to develop a handbook for parents on how they can help the class or school. A full range of items should be included.

School/home notes are useful when daily contact is warranted due to a student's ongoing behavioral or academic problems. The note is a two-way communication device that serves as a daily "report card" on the student's activities. The frequency of feedback that both you and the parents receive is maximized and issues can be dealt with quickly, which enhances your overall effectiveness. You can benefit from the parents' information on what skills the students have and what skills need to be taught, while parents can provide extra practice on skills at home and teach new ones.

The school note functions best as part of a "contract" contingency, with rewards for school behavior being given at home based on classroom task completion or other predetermined criteria. Parents have more time and resources at their disposal as well as the strongest relationship with the child in general, so it stands to reason that they can place the most powerful contingencies on the child with the best chances for skill generalization (Kelley, 1990).

Communication among parents and the school staff is critical if a school note program is to succeed. A school note program should not be initiated without parental involvement or consent, or all may be for naught; in fact, a teacher may be viewed as punitive. When teachers and parents do meet to determine the goals of the school note, it is important to keep the focus narrow and to concentrate on one to three behaviors at a time. The teacher should be told what reinforcers and consequences are associated with the note. The teacher is then responsible for filling out the note contingently and consistently, always noting more positive than negative behaviors. Any design may be used as long as it is easy to read, specific, and quick to fill out. Sample school notes are shown in Figures 1 and 2.

Parental involvement means more than helping students at home. The notion of parents as teachers holds great promise and may take many forms, including school tutors and classroom volunteers. Parents often have many unique abilities that can be tapped for educational purposes, but the school must first be an inviting environment in order to stimulate interest. Parents should be involved with the school community on all levels, e.g., decision-making teams, district-wide committees, room parents, parent-teacher organizations, etc. In order to inform parents of what is available, it's best to encourage them to come to the school freely. Providing opportunities such as curriculum nights, sharing school lunch with their children, and open classroom policies encourage visits from the parents.

The school as a community building is a concept gaining more popularity and attention, as well as the teacher visiting the students' homes. Surveying parents about the ways they would like to be involved in the school program is probably the best method of determining how they would like their needs to be met. A sample survey can be found in Figure 3 (Lyons, Robbins, & Smith, 1983).

A recommended practice for all school programs is the use of self-evaluation to determine if the community's needs are being met. Conducting parent consumer questionnaires can provide schools with much needed feedback from the parents' perspective and improve community relationships as a result. Figure 4 is a sample parent consumer questionnaire.

Teachers must have a community-oriented spirit if working with parents is to be a positive experience, and that spirit begins by having a positive and open attitude with the children in the classroom. It is of great benefit to teach a unit on how people differ early in the year and to model the appreciation of others' unique properties. Difference is not merely viewed as a cultural agenda but also that of family structures (Olson, 1994). When individuals do not acknowledge differences, they tend to evaluate others based on the dominant culture's standards instead of interpreting behavior based on a family's values and priorities. Decisions about what is best for a child may be based on inaccurate or biased information (Sontag & Schacht, 1994). However, when differences are taught as strengths, intercultural parity results, and in the classroom "family" each student becomes equal in value.

Figure 1 (front)

School Note

NAME_____ DATE _____

(Teachers please initial all entries)

Class	Responsible Behaviors	Irresponsible Behaviors
1		
2		
3		
4		
5		
6		
7		

Target Behaviors:

1. Follows instructions
2. Obtains permission
3. Uses greeting skills
4. Accepts criticism
5. Uses appropriate language
6. Stays on task
7. Completes assignments
8. Participates in class
9. Arrives on time
10. Volunteers
11. Personal appearance
12. Has necessary supplies
13. _____
14. _____

Period	Homework Assignment	T.I.
1		
2		
3		
4		
5		
6		
7		

Figure 1 (back)

School Staff Comments

This student did well in the following areas... (Include items of **EXTRA EFFORT** in both social and academic areas.) Please initial.

_____

_____

_____

_____

_____

_____

_____

_____

We need to help the student improve in the following areas... (Include major social and academic problems, and any referrals to the Principal.) Please initial.

_____

_____

_____

_____

_____

Additional information (for use by parents and school staff).

_____

_____

_____

_____

_____

(Parent Signature)

Figure 2

Cindy's School Note

Date: _____ **Mon.**   **Tues.**   **Wed.**   **Thurs.**   **Fri.**

My Behavior	During School	After School
I kept my hands and feet to myself.	yes ___ no ___	yes ___ no ___
I worked hard on my schoolwork and stayed on-task.	yes ___ no ___	yes ___ no ___
I talked respectfully to my teachers and followed their instructions.	yes ___ no ___	yes ___ no ___
My teacher's initials:	_____	_____
Any other comments:		

Figure 3

Parent Involvement Program Survey

Name _____ Phone _____

Address _____

Children in School(s)

Name of Child	Age	School

I would like to learn more about:

___ things I can do to help my child in school.
___ how to help in the school and classroom.

I would be interested in:

___ just getting to know more parents in the community.
___ being in a fun group that gets me out of the house.
___ craft classes.
___ learning more about what's going on in the community for me and my family.

If a group of parents got together, I would like to talk about:

___ ways to talk and listen to my children and work out problems.
___ ways to get my children to do what they need to do.
___ ways to manage so that my children get good food and health care.
___ ways to feel more comfortable talking with teachers, counselors, doctors, nurses... all the people who work with my children.
___ ways to deal with living in a community of many different cultures and a chance to learn more about each other.
___ ways to deal with my children about big things like life, death, love, sex, work, responsibility, education, money, trust, honesty, prejudice, drugs, alcohol, etc.

I could go to meetings:

___ in the morning.
___ in the afternoon.
___ in the evening.
___ on weekends.

I think the best place for parents to get together is:

___ in a home.
___ at the school.
___ community center/library.
___ other: _____

Return this form to your child's teacher by: _____

From Lyons, P., Robbins, A., & Smith, A. (1983). *Involving Parents: A Handbook for Participation in Schools*, pp. 168-69.

Figure 4

Parent Interview

School: _____ Date: _____

Please use the following scale to indicate your level of agreement with the statements listed below.

7 = Strongly Agree
6 = Agree
5 = Slightly Agree
4 = Neither Agree nor Disagree
3 = Slightly Disagree
2 = Disagree
1 = Strongly Disagree

1. My child's teacher is friendly and pleasant to talk with. _____
Comments:

2. My child's teacher is concerned and wants my child to do well in school. _____
Comments:

3. My child is treated fairly by teachers and administrators. _____
Comments:

4. I've been kept well informed about my child's progress at school. _____
Comments:

5. My child's teacher expects students to behave well in class. _____
Comments:

Figure 4 (continued)

6. My child's teacher runs a well-controlled classroom where learning can occur. _____

Comments:

7. The discipline used at school is effective in helping to change behavior. _____

Comments:

8. When my child has difficulty, his/her teacher is aware and provides special help. _____

Comments:

9. My child is learning important social skills and behavior (such as following instructions, disagreeing appropriately, etc.) which will help him/her later in life. _____

Comments:

10. My child is making nice progress in his/her behavior at school. _____

Comments:

11. My child likes his/her teacher and enjoys going to school. _____

Comments:

12. My child is making nice progress with his/her schoolwork. _____

Comments:

▶ Roadblocks to parent involvement

Teachers may have the best intentions to help children succeed in school, and in fact may have put forth a great deal of effort to involve parents and keep them informed. Sometimes our best efforts are to no avail due to family problems over which we have no control. Some of those problems and suggestions include:

1. Apathy. When it appears that parents have given up on their children and make statements to that regard, it is important to say and do things that model hopefulness. The teacher can also make an impact by reinforcing any enthusiasm or interest and by asking questions or making comments that may bring out positive responses.

2. Unreliable parents. The best approach with parents who seem to be unreliable is to use preventive and educational methods. That is, let parents know what you need, and when and why you need it. Prior to labeling a parent as unreliable, however, efforts should be made to determine if there is an underlying reason. Often, jobs and finances may preclude classroom volunteering or conference attendance, which may be misread as disinterest (Olson, 1994). Parents also may lack transportation or child care. Teachers must provide alternative solutions if this is the case, such as meeting with the parents at their homes or holding telephone meetings. Some parents who have had negative school experiences may not feel welcome or may feel intimidated. When individuals feel they have nothing to contribute, it is difficult for them to be motivated. It is important to be welcoming and reinforcing and offer parents meaningful roles with which they are comfortable. Language barriers also may prevent involvement; therefore, every effort to communicate in a parent's first language should be made.

3. Hostile and uncooperative parents. When faced with an angry person, it is imperative to remain calm and professional. Emphasizing a problem-solving mode of thinking while expressing empathy may defuse the situation, but the meeting may need to be brought to a close and an administrator may need to be present at any subsequent meetings for mediation purposes. Teachers should always monitor their behavior and ask for feedback if warranted. Telling parents that their input is valued may help, as well. If a teacher determines that a parent is intoxicated, he or she should not try to reason with the parent, but should end the conversation tactfully and as quickly as possible. Do not get into a situation that is potentially physically threatening. Ask for administrative assistance.

4. Severe personal problems of parents. This is a difficult area to change due to the lack of control that teachers have over parents' behavior. Resist the urge to act as a counselor except to refer parents to a school social worker who may be able to tell them about public and private agencies that are able to provide services. The full service school where families can receive appropriate intervention is perhaps not far down the road. Even though teachers are not therapists, the children should be given as much empathy and support as is warranted.

5. Abusive and neglectful parents. When discovered, abuse and neglect must be reported to the appropriate state agencies. To ensure that the school is a safe environment for children, policies and procedures should be followed to the letter.

▶ Summary

Schools and teachers have been charged with the responsibility of increasing parental involvement in their programs. It is agreed that children simply do better when their parents are involved, but both adult factions are faced with limited time and resources with which to get the job done. If we are to improve the quality of education for children in the 21st century, we must overcome some of the seemingly insurmountable barriers. As is stated in an African proverb, "It takes an entire village to raise a child."

Concluding Thoughts

The Boys Town Education Model is a comprehensive, systematic method of teaching prosocial skills to and building relationships with youth. Its four components – the Social Skills Curriculum, Teaching Interactions, Motivation Systems, and Administrative Intervention – help students learn productive ways of managing their own behavior and interacting with others. It combines the best of skill-based teaching with care and concern, resulting in improvements in students' behavior, self-esteem, and relationships with others.

By implementing this Model into your school, you can help ensure a quality Catholic education to every student in your care. It also is essential for the Catholic education community to develop general criteria that integrate the cultural, social, civil, pedagogical, and political aspects of school life in each child's daily instruction. The Congregation for Catholic Education outlined these criteria:

a) Fidelity to the Gospel as proclaimed by the Church. The activity of a Catholic school is, above all else, an activity that shares in the evangelizing mission of the Church; it is a part of the particular local Church of the country in which it is situated, and shares in the life and work of the local Christian community.

b) Careful rigor in the study of culture and the development of a critical sense, maintaining a respect for the autonomy of human knowledge and for the rules and methods proper to each of the disciplines, and at the same time orienting the whole process toward the integral information of the person.

c) Adapting the educational process in a way that respects the particular circumstances of individual students and their families.

d) Sharing responsibility with the Church. While school authorities are the ones primarily responsible for the educational and cultural activities of the school, the local Church should also be involved in appropriate ways; the educational goal should be the result of dialogue with this ecclesial community. (The Religious Dimension of Education in a Catholic school, 101)

Catholic schools have always faced a tremendous challenge. Not only are they responsible for the academic and emotional development of children, but they also must incorporate the spiritual and religious dimension that is essential to an education in the Catholic faith.

There also is a need for children to be equipped with a moral compass that will enable them to make the distinction between right and wrong as they solve problems and make decisions in their lives. Teaching students social skills and building relationships with them are important and effective ways to achieve this goal. The competition for a child's spiritual self is fierce. In order to win this battle, teachers must use every means at their disposal to steer their students away from the many temptations they face into today's world.

"Examine all things, hold onto what is good."

Thessalonians 5:21

Social skills for students

Basic skills

Skill 1

Following instructions

1. Look at the person.
2. Say "Okay."
3. Do what you've been asked right away.
4. Check back.

Skill 2

Accepting criticism or a consequence

1. Look at the person.
2. Say "Okay."
3. Don't argue.

Skill 3

Accepting "No" for an answer

1. Look at the person.
2. Say "Okay."
3. Stay calm.
4. If you disagree, ask later.

Skill 4

Greeting others

1. Look at the person.
2. Use a pleasant voice.
3. Say "Hi" or "Hello."

Skill 5

Getting the teacher's attention

1. Look at the teacher.
2. Raise your hand. Stay calm.
3. Wait until the teacher says your name.
4. Ask your question.

Skill 6

Making a request

1. Look at the person.
2. Use a clear, pleasant voice.
3. Explain exactly what you are asking for. Say "Please."
4. If the answer is "Yes," say "Thank you."
5. If not, remember to accept "No" for an answer.

Skill 7

Disagreeing appropriately

1. Look at the person.
2. Use a pleasant voice.
3. Say "I understand how you feel."
4. Tell why you feel differently.
5. Give a reason.
6. Listen to the other person.

Advanced skills

Skill 8

Giving criticism

1. Look at the person.
2. Stay calm. Use a pleasant voice.
3. Say something positive, or "I understand."
4. Describe exactly what you are criticizing.
5. Tell why this is a problem.
6. Listen to the person. Be polite.

Skill 9

Resisting peer pressure

1. Look at the person.
2. Use a calm voice.
3. Say clearly that you do not want to participate.
4. Suggest something else to do.
5. If necessary, continue to say "No."
6. Leave the situation.

Skill 10

Making an apology

1. Look at the person.
2. Use a serious, sincere voice.
3. Say "I'm sorry for... " or "I want to apologize for...."
4. Don't make excuses.
5. Explain how you plan to do better in the future.
6. Say "Thanks for listening."

Skill 11

Talking with others

1. Look at the person.
2. Use a pleasant voice.
3. Ask questions.
4. Don't interrupt.

Skill 12

Giving compliments

1. Look at the person.
2. Smile.
3. Speak clearly and enthusiastically.
4. Tell the person exactly what you like.

Skill 13

Accepting compliments

1. Look at the person.
2. Use a pleasant voice.
3. Say "Thank you."
4. Don't look away, mumble, or refuse the compliment.
5. Do not disagree with the compliment.

Skill 14

Volunteering

1. Look at the person.
2. Use a pleasant, enthusiastic voice.
3. Ask if you can help. Describe the activity or task you are offering to do.
4. Thank the person.
5. Check back when you have finished.

Skill 15

Reporting other youths' behavior

1. Look at the teacher or adult.
2. Use a calm voice. Ask to talk to him or her privately.
3. Describe the inappropriate behavior you are reporting.
4. Explain why you are making the report.
5. Answer any questions the adult has.
6. Thank the adult for listening.

Skill 16

Introducing yourself

1. Look at the person. Smile.
2. Use a pleasant voice.
3. Offer a greeting. Say "Hi, my name is...."
4. Shake the person's hand.
5. When you leave, say, "It was nice to meet you."

References

Alberto, P.A., & Troutmann, A.C. (1990). **Applied behavior analysis for teachers** (3rd ed.). Columbus, OH: Merrill Publishing Company.

Anderson, L., Evertson, C., & Emmer, E. (1980). Dimensions in classroom management derived from recent research. **Journal of Curriculum Studies, 12**, 343-356.

Aspy, D., & Roebuck, R. (1977). **Kids don't learn from people they don't like**. Amherst, MA: Human Resource Development Press.

Bandura, A. (1969). **Principles of behavior modification**. New York: Holt, Rinehart & Winston.

Bandura, A. (1977). **Social learning theory**. Englewood Cliffs, NJ: Prentice-Hall.

Baron, R.L., Cunningham, P.J., Palma, L.P., & Phillips, E.L. (1984). **Family and community living skills curriculum** (rev. ed.). Boys Town, NE: Father Flanagan's Boys' Home.

Becker, W., Engelmann, S., & Thomas, D., (1975). **Teaching 1: Classroom management**. Chicago: Research Press.

Betty Phillips Center for Parenthood Education (1992). **Parent involvement report, 2,**1. Nashville, TN: Peabody College, Vanderbilt University.

Bluestein, J. (1988). 21st century discipline: **Teaching students responsibility and self-control**. Jefferson City, MO: Scholastic Inc.

Borich, G.D. (1971). Accountability in the affective domain. **Journal of Research and Development in Education, 5**, 87-96.

Braukmann, P.D., Ramp, K.K., Braukmann, C.J., Willner, A.G., & Wolf, M.M. (1983). The analysis and training of rationales for child care workers. **Children and Youth Services Review, 5**, 177-194.

Bronfenbrenner, U. (1970). **Two worlds of childhood: U.S. and U.S.S.R.** New York: Russell Sage.

Brophy, J. (1983). Research on the self-ful-filling prophecy and teacher expectations. **Journal of Educational Psychology, 75**, 631-661.

Brown, L.J., Black, D.D., & Downs, J.C. (1984). **School social skills rating scale and manual**. East Aurora, NY: Slosson Educational Publications.

Burch, P., & Palanki, A. (1994) Parent-teacher action research: Supporting families through family-school-community part-nerships. **Journal of Emotional and Behavioral Problems, 2**(4).

Bush, R. (1954). **The teacher-pupil relation-ship**. Englewood Cliffs, NJ: Prentice-Hall.

Cartledge, G., & Milburn, J.F. (1978). The case of teaching social skills in the classroom: A review. **Review of Educational Research, 1**, 133-156.

Charles, C. (1989). **Building classroom disci-pline: From models to practice** (3rd ed.). New York: Longman.

Clark, H.B., Wood, R., & Northrop, J. (1980). The family and education: New direc-tions for promoting healthy social interac-tions. In J.B. Gordon, D.A. Sabatino, & R. C. Sarri (Eds.), **Disruptive youth in school** (pp. 151-172). Reston, VA: Council for Exceptional Children.

Combs, M.L., & Slaby, D.A. (1977). Social skills training with children. In B.B. Lahey & A.E. Kazdin (Eds.), **Advances in clinical child psychology** (pp. 161-201). New York: Plenum Press.

Cooper, J.O., Heron, T.E., & Heward, W.L. (1987). **Applied behavior analysis**. Columbus, OH: Merrill Publishing Company.

Cormany, R. (1975). **Guidance and coun-seling in Pennsylvania: Status and needs**. Lemoyne, PA: ESEA Title II Project, West Shore School District.

Coughlin, D.D., Maloney, D.M., Baron, R.L., Dahir, J., Daly, D.L., Daly, P.B., Fixsen, D.L., Phillips, E.L., & Thomas, D.L. (1983). Implementing the community-based Teaching-Family Model at Boys Town. In W.P. Christian, G.T. Hanna, & T.J. Glahon (Eds.), **Programming effective human services: Strategies for institutional change and client transition**. New York: Plenum Press.

Czerwionka, J. (1987). **Influences of struc-tured learning on the prosocial behavior of behaviorally disordered adolescents**. Unpublished doctoral dissertation. Dekalb, IL: Northern Illinois University.

Damon, W. (1988). **The moral child: Nurturing children's natural moral growth**. New York: The Free Press.

DeRisi, W.J., & Butz, G. (1975). **Writing behavioral contracts: A case simulation practice manual**. Champaign, IL: Research Press.

Dowd, T., & Tierney, J. (1992). **Teaching social skills to youth: A curriculum for child-care providers**. Boys Town, NE: Boys Town Press.

Downs, J.C., Bastien, J., Brown, L.J., & Wells, P.L. (1987). **Motivation systems workshop manual** (rev. ed.). Boys Town, NE: Father Flanagan's Boys' Home.

Downs, J., Kutsick, K., & Black, D. (1985). The teaching interaction: A systematic approach to developing social skills in disruptive and non-disruptive students. **Techniques: A Journal for Remedial Education and Counseling, 1**, 304-310.

Doyle, W. (1986). Classroom organization and management. In M.C. Wittrock (Ed.), **Handbook of research on teaching** (3rd ed.). New York: MacMillan.

Duke, D., & Meckel, A. (1984). **Teacher's guide to classroom management**. New York: Random House.

D'Zurilla, T.J., & Goldfried, M.R. (1971). Problem solving and behavior modification. **Journal of Abnormal Psychology, 78**, 107-126.

Elder, G.H., Jr. (1963). Parental power legitimation and its effect on adolescents. **Sociometry, 26**, 50-65.

Father Flanagan's Boys' Home (1991). **Boys Town Family Home Program training manual** (3rd ed.). Boys Town, NE: Author.

Goldstein, A.P. (1988). **The prepare curriculum: Teaching prosocial competencies**. Champaign, IL: Research Press.

Goldstein, A.P., Sprafkin, R.P., Gershaw, N.J., & Klein, P. (1980). The adolescent: Social skills training through structured learning. In G. Cartledge & J.F. Milburn (Eds.), **Teaching social skills to children**. New York: Pergamon Press.

Gresham, F.M. (1981). Assessment of children's social skills. **Journal of School Psychology, 19**(2), 120-133.

Gresham, F.M. (1982). Misguided mainstreaming: The case for social skills training with handicapped children. **Exceptional Children, 48**(5), 422-433.

Grosenick, J.K., & Huntze, S.L. (Eds.) (1984). **National needs analysis in behavior disorders: Positive alternatives to disciplinary exclusion**. Columbia, MO: University of Missouri, Department of Special Education.

Hansen, D., St. Lawrence, J., & Christoff, K. (1980). Conversational skills of inpatient conduct disordered youth. **Behavior Modification, 12**(3), 424-444.

Hope, H., & Cobb, J.A. (1973). Survival behaviors in the educational setting: Their implications for research and intervention. In L.A. Hammerlynk, L.C. Hanay, & E.J. Mash (Eds.), **Behavior change** (pp. 193-208). Champaign, IL: Research Press.

Jones, M., & Offord, D. (1989). Reduction of antisocial behavior in poor children by nonschool skill-development. **Journal of Child Psychology and Psychiatry, 30**(5), 737-750.

Jones, V.F., & Jones, L.S. (1981). **Responsible classroom discipline: Creating positive learning environments and solving problems**. Boston: Allyn and Bacon, Inc.

Jones, V.F., & Jones, L.S. (1990). **Comprehensive classroom management: Motivating and managing students** (3rd ed.). Boston: Allyn and Bacon.

Kaplan, J. (1991). **Beyond behavior modification**. Austin, TX: Pro-Ed.

Kaplan, J.S. (1991). **Beyond behavior modification** (2nd ed.). Austin, TX: Pro-Ed.

Kelley, M.L. (1990). **School-home notes: Promoting children's classroom success**. New York: Guilford Press.

Kendall, P., & Braswell, L. (1982). Cognitive-behavioral self-control therapy for children: A components analysis. **Journal of Consulting & Clinical Psychology, 50**, 672-689.

Kounin, J. (1970). **Discipline and group management in classrooms**. New York: Holt, Rinehart, and Winston.

Kuykendall, K. (1992). **From rage to hope: Strategies for reclaiming black and Hispanic students**. Bloomington, IN: National Educational Services.

Larson, K. (1989). Task-related and interpersonal problem-solving training for increasing school success in high-risk young adolescents. **Remedial and Special Education, 20**, 244-253.

Liturgy Training Publications (1996). **The catechetical documents: A parish resource**. Chicago: Author.

Mager, R.F. (1992). **No skill-efficacy, no performance**. Training, (4), 32-36.

Miller, C.S. (1984). Building self-control. **Young Children**, 15-19.

Montague, M. (1988). Job-related social skills training for adolescents with handicaps. **Career Development for Exceptional Individuals, 11**(1), 26-41.

Morse, W. (1964). Self-concept in the school setting. **Childhood Education, 41**, 195-198.

Mortimore, P., & Sammons, P. (1987). New evidence on effective elementary schools. **Educational Leadership, 45**, 4-8.

Nichols, P. (1992). The curriculum of control: Twelve reasons for it, some arguments against it. **Beyond Behavior**, Winter, 5-11.

Norman, J., & Harris, M. (1981). **The private life of the American teenager**. New York: Rawson, Wade.

Northwest Regional Education Laboratory (1990). Effective schooling practices: A research synthesis. In **Onward to Excellence**. Portland, OR: Author.

O'Leary, K.D., & Drabman, R. (1971). Token reinforcement programs in the classroom: A review. **Psychological Bulletin, 75**, 379-398.

Olson, M. (1994). Five ways teachers can help children from single parent families. **Journal of Emotional and Behavioral Problems, 2**(4).

Peter, V.J. (1986). **What makes Boys Town so special?** Boys Town, NE: Father Flanagan's Boys' Home.

Phillips, E.L. (1968). Achievement place: Token reinforcement procedures in a home-style rehabilitation setting for "predelinquent" boys. **Journal of Applied Behavior Analysis, 1**, 213-223.

Phillips, E.L., Phillips, E.A., Fixsen, D.L., & Wolf, M.M. (1974). **The Teaching-Family handbook** (rev. ed.). Lawrence, KS: University of Kansas Printing Service.

Pikas, A. (1961). Children's attitudes toward rational versus inhibiting parental authority. **Journal of Abnormal Social Psychology, 62,** 313-321.

Porter, A., & Brophy, J. (1988). Synthesis of research on good teaching. **Educational Leadership, 45,** 74-85.

Purkey, W., & Novak, J. (1984). **Inviting school success: A self-concept approach to teaching and learning** (2nd ed.). Belmont, CA: Wadsworth.

Rhode, G., Jensen, W.R., & Reavis, H.K. (1992). **The tough kid book: Practical classroom management strategies.** Longmont, CO: Sopris West.

Roosa, J.B. (1973). **SOCS: Situations, options, consequences, simulations: A technique for teaching social interactions.** Unpublished paper presented to the American Psychological Association, Montreal.

Rosenshine, B. (1970). Enthusiastic teaching: A research review. **School Review, 72,** 449-514.

Sanford, J., Emmer, E., & Clements, B. (1983). Improving classroom managment. **Educational Leadership, 41,** 56-60.

Sarason, I.G. (1968). Verbal learning, modeling, and juvenile delinquency. **American Psychologist, 23,** 254-266.

Schneider, B.H., & Byrne, B.M. (1984). Predictors of successful transition from self-contained special education to regular class settings. **Psychology in the Schools, 21,** 375-380.

Schumaker, J.B., Hazel, J.S., Sherman, J.S., & Sheldon, J. (1982). Social skill performance of learning disabled, non-learning disabled, and delinquent adolescents. **Learning Disabilities Quarterly, 5,** 388-397.

Serow, R.C., & Soloman, D. (1979). Classroom climates and students' intergroup behavior. **Journal of Educational Psychology, 71,** 669-676.

Shah, S.A. (1966). **A behavioral conceptualization of the development of criminal behavior, therapeutic principles, and applications.** A Report to the President's Commission on Law Enforcement and the Administration of Justice. Washington, DC: U.S. Government Printing Office.

Shah, S.A. (1968). Preparation for release and community follow-up. In H.L. Cohen, A.L. Cohen, I. Goldiamond, J. Filipczak, & R. Pooley (Eds.), **Training professionals in procedures for the establishment of educational environments.** Silver Springs, MD: Institute for Behavioral Research, Educational Facility Press.

Shores, R.E., Gunter, P.L., & Jack, S.L. (1993). Classroom management strategies: Are they setting event for coercion? **Behavior Disorders, 18,** 92-102.

Smallwood, D.L., Hawryluk, M.K., & Pierson, E. (1990). Promoting parent involvement in schools to serve at-risk students. In Kruger, L.J. (Ed.), **Promoting success with at-risk students: Emerging perspectives and practical approaches.** New York: Haworth Press.

Sontag, J.C., & Schacht, R. (1994). An ethnic comparison of parent participation and information needs in early intervention. **Exceptional Children, 60**(5), 422-433.

Spivack, G., & Schure, M.B. (1974). **Social adjustment of young children**. San Francisco: Jossey-Bass.

Steinberg, Z. (1992). Pandora's children. **Beyond Behavior**, Spring, 5-13.

Steinberg, Z., & Knitzer, J. (1992). Classrooms for emotionally and behaviorally disturbed students: Facing the challenge. **Behavioral Disorders, 17**(2), 145-156.

Stephens, T.M. (1978). **Social skills in the classroom**. Columbus, OH: Cedar Press, Inc.

Stephens, T.M., & Wolf, J.S. (1980). **Effective skills in parent and teacher conferencing**. National Center for Educational Materials and Media for the Handicapped, Columbus, OH: Ohio State University.

United States Department of Education (1989). **Eleventh annual report to Congress on the implementation of the Education of the Handicapped Act**. Washington, DC: Author.

United States Department of Education (1993). **Goals 2000: Educate America Act 1993**. Washington, DC: Author.

Venziano, C., & Venziano, L. (1988). Knowledge of social skills among institutionalized juvenile delinquents. **Criminal Justice and Behavior, 15**(2), 152-171.

White, O.R., & Haring, N.G. (1980). **Exceptional teaching** (2nd ed.). Columbus, OH: Merrill Publishing Company.

Willner, A.G., Braukmann, C.J., Kirigin, K.A., Fixsen, D.L., Phillips, E.L., & Wolf, M.M. (1977). The training and validation of youth-preferred social behaviors of child care personnel. **Journal of Applied Behavior Analysis, 10**(2), 219-230.

Wolf, M.M., Phillips, E.L., & Fixsen, D.L. (1972). The Teaching-Family: A new model for the treatment of deviant child behavior in the community. In S.W. Bijou & E.L. Ribes-Inesta (Eds.), **Behavior modification: Issues and extensions** (pp. 51-62). New York: Academic Press.

Wolfgang, C., & Glickman, C. (1986). **Solving discipline problems: Strategies for classroom teachers** (2nd ed.). Boston: Allyn & Bacon.

■Index